HENRY MORSE

Translated by Philip Caraman

JOHN GERARD
THE AUTOBIOGRAPHY OF AN ELIZABETHAN

WILLIAM WESTON
THE AUTOBIOGRAPHY OF AN ELIZABETHAN

Multituds flying from London by water in boats & barges.

Flying by land.

Burying the dead with a bell before them.   Searchers.

Carts full of dead to bury.

PLAGUE SCENES

HENRY MORSE

Priest of the Plague

by

PHILIP CARAMAN

FARRAR, STRAUS AND CUDAHY
NEW YORK

NOTE

THE sources of this biography are given, according to chapters, at the end of the book. They are listed in such a way that the reader will be able to trace there every quotation in the text. For the genealogy of Fr. Henry Morse and for the information drawn from the wills of his family I am indebted to my friends, Mr. David Morse and Miss Enid Morse, and to Mrs. Warren R. Smith of Washington, D.C. I am also most deeply grateful to Miss C. V. Wedgwood, who read this book in typescript and suggested a number of changes, which I have done my best to carry out.

P.C.

CONTENTS

		Page
1	EARLY YEARS	1
2	FIRST IMPRISONMENT	10
3	ROME	16
4	ST. ANTHONY'S	28
5	THE SEA HORSE	41
6	YORK GAOL	53
7	FLANDERS	60
8	ST. GILES-IN-THE-FIELDS	68
9	PRIEST OF THE PLAGUE	77
10	THE DYING AND THE DEAD	86
11	INCREASE AND DECLINE	99
12	AT THE SIGN OF THE SUN	115
13	OLD BAILEY	124
14	ARCHBISHOP LAUD	136
15	CHAPLAIN IN THE FIELD	148
16	LAST ARREST	157
17	NEWGATE	168
18	TYBURN	179
	APPENDICES	
	A. NOTE ON ILLUSTRATIONS	187
	B. SOURCES	188
	INDEX	195

PLATES

PLAGUE SCENES   *Frontispiece*
    From a print at Magdalene College, Cambridge
    By kind permission of the Master and Fellows

                                          Facing page
HENRY MORSE   32
    From an engraved portrait in *Certamen Triplex*
    (1645)
    By kind permission of the Rector of Stonyhurst

NEWCASTLE-UPON-TYNE IN THE REIGN OF QUEEN
    ELIZABETH   33
    *By kind permission of Messrs. Andrew Reid & Co.,
    Newcastle-upon-Tyne*

TO THE CATHOLICKES OF ENGLAND   80
    From an original sheet in the Bodleian Library,
    Oxford
    By kind permission of the Bodleian Library

AN APOTHECARY'S SHOP AND A DOCTOR'S
    DISPENSARY   81
    From prints in the British Museum
    By kind permission of the Trustees

PLAGUE SCENES   112, 113
    From a pictorial broadside (1665) in the London
    Museum
    By kind permission of the Trustees

I

EARLY YEARS

THE third winter of the war had been severe, and London, cut off from its supply of coal by the Royalists holding Newcastle, had suffered bitterly. Trade was languid, and any small excitement in the streets drew out even larger crowds now that Parliament had prohibited bear-baiting and other forms of sport in a campaign to make Londoners more godly. Already at nine-thirty on an overcast morning the lanes, still muddy after a day and night of incessant rain, were lined with citizens of every class as a sledge, drawn by four horses, hurried through Newgate, across the river Fleet and along Holborn towards the Oxford road.

A spectator awaiting the arrival of the hurdle at Tyburn village described the crowd gathered there as 'almost infinite'. Perhaps fifty thousand were present, and watched a middle-aged man, with sunken sallow features, tall forehead and short pointed beard matted with fresh mud, untrussed from the crate and assisted up the ladder to a cart stationed beneath the gallows. The hangman fastened the noose, and then the criminal began the speech that long custom had established as his privilege. He chose his words with precision, made some fine legal points, referred to his work in London during the recent plague, and, like so many other priests before him, professed his innocence of any treacherous action against the King or Parliament.

Without emotion he declared that he had waited thirty years
for this very moment; but the words were not understood by
the crowd, and, while they still argued over their meaning, a
crack of a whip jerked the cart from under him and he was left
suspended against the grey January sky. An urchin leapt forward, caught his feet and swung himself to and fro. Before the
child was beaten off, the priest was dead.

It was the last execution that morning. The crowd returned
to their business. For the second time the Commons discussed
the raising of a new model army, to consist of six hundred
horse and fourteen hundred foot under the command of Sir
Thomas Fairfax. At the Guildhall the Lord Mayor drafted a
letter for presentation to the Master Speaker urging the re-
establishment of Lenten observance. Although some feared
that 'it looked too much to Rome', still it was reckoned that
the re-enforcement of Lent would bring 'a twofold benefit, as
well civil as divine, as well for the increase of the flesh of cattle
as for the subduing of the corruptions of our own': for the
fisheries were depressed and the stocks of cattle greatly reduced
by three years of war.

The execution was soon forgotten. The criminal had
behaved with dignity: and moreover there were trials pending
that gave promise of a more exciting end. The Lord Macguire,
now in Newgate, was bigger fry than a common Jesuit. There
were also spies ready soon for hanging in Smithfield. A more
startling confession might be expected from them, for Thomas
Baisty had made bullets for the Royalists besieged in Winchester House, and Beazly, the porter from the Ram in Smithfield, had reported to the King at Christ Church the movements
of the Parliamentary troops outside Oxford. If the sheriff
allowed them time to speak, their life-story would provide
more interest than a priest's brief account of his conversion,
exile and imprisonment.

.   .   .   .   .

Although London had once known him well, Henry Morse on the day of his execution was a stranger to the crowd, save to some of the poorer people from the outer suburbs of Holborn and Bloomsbury. The last five years he had passed partly in Flanders and partly in the extreme north of England. In the same month that Newcastle fell to the combined force of Scots and Roundheads, he had been arrested and despatched from the newly fallen city to London in a freighter that sailed in the first convoy to bring coals to the capital.

He was born in 1595 in the house of his mother, Margaret Collinson, at Broome, a small Suffolk village lying between Eye and Diss, less than a mile south of the Norfolk border. It has been claimed that he was connected with William Morse, twice Master of Trinity Hall, Cambridge, who, like his more famous contemporary, Andrew Perne of Peterhouse, trimmed his opinions to suit the prevailing religious fashion, and, after affecting fervent Catholicism under Mary, climbed high in the ecclesiastical world in the reign of Elizabeth. More probably he was a nephew of Thomas Morse, the Suffolk gentleman whose early career followed the same course as his own—Cambridge and the Inns of Court. Thomas was at Emmanuel in the late 'eighties—a contentious character, several times admonished for fighting and injuring his fellow-scholar, Sir James Fawether, in the college kitchen. The connection, however, cannot be established, for Morse was a common name in East Anglia, and had been long enshrined in the adage, 'He caught him napping as Morse did his horse'—a phrase used cynically by country-folk of a man caught in an attempt to do down his fellows. From a will proved in the Consistory Court of Norwich it can be shown that Henry was the son of Robert Morse of Tivetshall, a man of sufficient rents and land to leave a fair inheritance to each of the fourteen children who survived him. Tivetshall, his father's home, on the Norfolk side of the border, was only a short distance from Broome, his mother's home, to the south of it; and this explains why his biographers name indifferently both counties as the place of his origin. Consistently Henry called himself a Norfolk man. He was the seventh son. It is not known whether he received his early education at home or in the Grammar School at Norwich, where, in the parish of All Saints, his father held the lease of several houses from the Dean and Chapter. When Henry was fifteen, his second brother, Lionell, died from some lingering disease. To each member of his numerous family the young man, who had recently taken his degree at Oxford, left some small possession. To his younger sisters, Margaret, Mary and Martha, his Bible and Dante's *Pathway* to be used in common between them; to John Sherwood, a Doctor of Medicine, married to his eldest sister, Anne, his books of physic, philosophy and logic; and to his younger brothers, Henry, Geoffrey, John and Edward, all his school books to be distributed at the discretion of Robert, his brother and executor. His 'watchers' and the poor of Eye were not forgotten. This was in September 1610. Henry was then fifteen. He had not yet entered Corpus Christi College, Cambridge.

Since the days of the mastership of Matthew Parker, later Archbishop of Canterbury, the College had prospered. Parker had ordered its finances, established two new fellowships, and provided at the same time a valuable library of manuscripts. As a Norfolk man, Parker had favoured men from his own county, and, as a fervent reformer, had given the college an uncompromising Protestant character. Indeed he had gone so far as to persuade the heralds to alter its coat of arms, for he rightly considered the pelican, feeding her young with her blood, to be symbolic of Christ in the Eucharist and an abominable relic of Catholic superstition. When Henry was admitted, the College was perhaps the most flourishing in the University. It provided for twelve Fellows and thirty-seven scholars, who, with the students and officers, formed a total scholastic body of one hundred and twenty-six. The Master, Dr. John Capcot, a 'great critic in the Latin and Greek tongues', was now 'macerated by his constant studying'. It was he who on 10 May 1612 made Henry a pensioner in lower commons, under the tutorship of Dr. Osborne.

It was twenty-two years since Thomas Morse had left Emmanuel for Gray's Inn, but the traditions of the University were unchanged. Though railing and revelling and climbing the College walls at night were still the most common offences, there was a new sport of 'making and letting off squibs' which called for special legislation by the Master. Henry's name does not occur in any account of escapades. He appears not to have engaged with other members of the College in the obscure pastime of 'pumping the skull twist' or to have ridden horses in Maytime in Mr. Wolfe's meadow, 'making some of them break out into the corn'. That he was hot-tempered, like Thomas, we know from his own confession and from his conduct at the English College; but he passed from Corpus Christi to Barnard's Inn without leaving his name in the Admonition Book of the College.

Morse was in his seventeenth year when he started the study of law—the age recommended by Augustine Baker, then a famous Bencher in the Temple, who was shortly to give up his practice to become a Benedictine monk. If a youth stayed longer at the University he ran the risk, in Baker's opinion, of unfitting himself for this 'harsh and barbarous study'; his wit became 'seasoned' with softer pursuits—poetry and oratory— and he lost the concentration required to 'fasten on to the law'. But Morse had not been long enough at Cambridge to develop the 'quaint wit' that Baker despised. Conceit in phrase or behaviour was not in keeping with his character: his Latin, like his English, was adequate but unornate; and to judge from the use he later made of his legal knowledge, he did more than 'nibble at the law' at the Inns. Industrious and unimaginative, he possessed the toughness which Baker demanded of the student if the law was to 'sharpen his understanding' and 'enable him for reasoning on other subjects'. Morse, indeed, is likely also to have followed the relaxations favoured by Baker, who 'frequently eased himself with the reading of some pleasant book', as the Comedies of Plautus and Terence or Erasmus' *Dialogues*; or, alternatively, attended comedies, carrying always in a pocket a book of law, 'which he might study when the play pleased him not'.

This was the hey-day of the legal profession, and the Inns of Court were more crowded than the Universities. Not all persevered; many, as Baker observed, merely 'loitered at the law' while 'few attained to it'. Sir Edward Coke, in temporary eclipse, was engaged on his *Institutions*, which he completed in 1615, twelve months after Morse had left England. Lord Ellesmere was then Chancellor and, like Coke, compiling legal treatises; Thomas Coventry was solicitor-general, and Sir Lawrence Tanfield was the most famous judge on the King's Bench—all of them men who became familiar to Morse in his regular attendance with the students at the cases in which the sages spoke. Often it happened that the trial of a priest roused scruples concerning his religion in a student's mind. Baker, we know, was present at the arraignment of most of the prisoners charged with treason, and 'perceived plainly that where the Prince is offended and for reasons of state will have any person or party traduced and punished', then the 'attorneys, sollicitors and great lawyers' affect anything to 'gratify the Prince'. In the joint trial of the three priests, William Scott, Richard Newport and John Almond, Coke had startled the court by stating that in the case of *praemunire* a man was judged guilty, if he neither owned nor denied the fact. It was a novel principle, and its acceptance by the court caused the death of the three priests. Possibly the long discussion which the sentence provoked gave Morse his first religious scruples. At the same time he may well have come under the Catholic influence which was always strong in the student societies. From the first days of the English counter-reformation Cardinal Allen had realised that the unscrupulous conduct of judges could be turned to the advantage of the Catholic cause. In a memorandum on the English mission he laid it down that, after the two Universities, the Inns provided the most promising source for converts. By personal intercourse and by books printed in Belgium and passed round among the students, he had observed that priests made 'wonderful headway'. For several decades in every hand-list of priests drawn up by spies, marked but untracked 'seminaries' are noted as 'being in the Inns of Court'. Few can be identified. But in Allen's own time it is known that John Hambley, a Douai-trained man, carried on a brief apostolate of five weeks before he was arrested at Mass in Gray's Inn, and so taken to prison with his 'vestments, wine and singing cake'.

However, 'lurking priests' remained a constant anxiety to the government, and the flow of converts continued. Many young men, perhaps Morse among them, left the Universities at sixteen, when the oath of allegiance was tendered, in order to continue their studies with undisturbed conscience in London.

But there is no record of the beginnings of religious doubt in Morse's mind. During his years at Barnard's Inn and later in the chambers of Mr. Richard Ross, a lawyer of Gray's Inn who was married to his cousin, he attended Anglican services irregularly but never once received the Sacrament. This was remarkable, for in 1610, by order of the King, all law students were compelled to receive the 'Supper of Calvin', which they did, often without conviction, 'some sitting, some walking, some kneeling, and with other signs of contempt'. Morse's refusal to make even a conventional act of conformity with the other students suggests that he had his first 'scruples' on leaving Cambridge. In July that year his father had died. Although there is no evidence in his will that Robert Morse became a Catholic, he had been in sympathy with the Church for many years. As early as March 1583 he had been delated to the Bishop's court at Norwich as a recusant attending 'secret Mass in the parlour at Stuston parsonage' and was reported also to have 'entertained' a priest called Montfort Scott, who was later executed. If he died a Catholic, then Henry may have had his first doubts at his father's deathbed. His own statement is vague. 'It happened that whilst I was a Protestant and studying in one of the Inns of Court at London, being agitated by scruples concerning the truth of my religion, I passed over into Belgium.' This was in May 1614. Almost a year earlier, in April 1613, William, his fifth brother, then in his twenty-second year, had given up the study of law in London to enter the seminary at Douai. This is the first known conversion in the large family. But it is likely that Robert, his third brother, had become a Catholic still earlier when he married Margaret, the daughter of Henry Bedingfeld, 'one of the most obstinate Papists' in Norfolk.

Henry crossed to the Continent via Gravesend. With a licence from the Privy Council to travel abroad, he had no need to pass secretly out of the country by a small south-coast port. Moreover, at this time stories were circulating in London of a man-eating dragon rampaging in the woods between London and the south. A warning to travellers was published in a curious pamphlet written in the August following Morse's departure. The monster was said to rove principally in St. Leonard's Forest. Nine feet or rather more in length, it was shaped like the axletree of a cart, thick in the middle and smaller at both ends. The author-witness, observing the beast from a 'reasonable ocular distance', reported that its belly was red and that black scales adorned its rump. 'At the sight or hearing of men or cattle he raised his neck arrogantly.' Two great swellings on either side, as 'big as a large football', were thought to be sprouting wings, and it was hoped that God would see that he was killed before he became fully-fledged. Already by throwing its venom four roods ahead of him, the beast had slain two mastiff dogs and several men and women.

Even in a credulous age such a rumour was unlikely to deter travellers from using the roads to the south-coast ports. It is improbable that dread of this monster determined Morse to sail from Gravesend. It was a common route to France, particularly for Londoners, although, in Fynes Moryson's experience, the town had little to commend it and gave such 'ill-entertainment' to travellers, both English and foreign, that few lodged there even for a night 'except upon necessity'.

From Dunkerque, the usual port of disembarkation, Morse proceeded to the English seminary at Douai. His arrival is recorded in the College Diary under 5 June 1614. There, 'having learnt the certain truth of the Catholic faith', he says, 'upon full conviction I renounced my former errors and was received into the Roman Catholic Church, the mistress of all Churches'.

2

FIRST IMPRISONMENT

FROM its foundation in 1568 the College at Douai had been the first Continental refuge for young Englishmen, seeking to settle in exile a conscience troubled by the claims of the old religion. Allen had welcomed them with sympathy, and the College's tradition of hospitality had been maintained by Dr. Matthew Kellison, who had been installed as fourth President in the November preceding Morse's arrival. A rubicund, humbly born man, 'above the common size, with a majestic carriage', he had been educated first in the household of Lord Vaux of Harrowden, where his father had been in service. Hiding great affability under a rough exterior, he was a type of church dignitary common in more quiet times. He was a forceful theologian, and his controversial works on Catholic doctrine, written when he was Regius professor of theology at Rheims University, had won him his present position. For twenty-seven years he governed the College firmly and ably, successfully training his young students for priestly work in England, although he himself had never worked there as a missionary. It was he who welcomed Morse as a 'convictor', the term used to denote paying residents at the College in distinction from the students on the foundation.

Significantly, on 11 June, less than a week after Morse's arrival, the return of his brother William is noted in the

College Diary. 'Certain business', perhaps Henry's conversion, had taken him to England in the previous September at the conclusion of his philosophical course. He had been absent the entire scholastic year; but he was on the Continent again in time to witness his brother's confirmation in the College chapel—the sacrament which was the external sign of his formal submission to the Church.

A few months later Henry set out for England, with the intention of settling his estate before starting his studies for the priesthood. In his will, proved on the feast of the Assumption, 1615, Robert Morse had made ample provision for his wife and all his fourteen children. Henry received no real estate. His father's land in the nearby village of Hoxne, settled on his wife at the time of their marriage, remained hers for life, while his tenements and leases in Norwich passed to his eldest son, Thomas; Robert, the second surviving son, received the close called Dowstoft in Tivetshall, a meadow called Holbeach, with two acres of copyhold land, the corn in his granaries, his cattle and instruments of husbandry. Henry, like William and Philip and his younger brothers Geoffrey and John, was left three hundred pounds and a further twenty-seven pounds a year.[1] And 'to Edith Syer, my loving sister', the will concluded, 'and to my loving cousin, Anne the wife of Mr. Richard Ross, two French crowns each, to make them rings for a remembrance of my goodwill'. Nor did Robert Morse forget the poor of St. Mary's and St. Margaret's in Tivetshall; they both received five pounds.

On deciding to become a priest Henry had to arrange for the secret transfer of his inheritance to the Continent. The College at Douai was poorly founded. Whenever it was possible the students contributed, in part at least, to their own expenses. In

[1] Under his father's will Henry received also 'the silver bell salt with a cover which was given unto him by his grandmother'.

Henry's case the money settled on him by his father was more than sufficient for his maintenance during his six years of study. The visit too would enable him to take farewell of his family. He proposed to be back in the autumn, when he could begin his course of philosophy at the same time as his brother William entered his first year of divinity.

Immediately on landing Henry was arrested. He was tendered the oath of allegiance, and refused to take it. It may have been at Dover that this mischance occurred. From the first days of the new religion the town, with all its neighbouring ports, had been almost brutally anti-Catholic. Only here in England was there any bitterness of religious feeling comparable to that of the French Huguenots, who alone of all the travellers who passed through the port, were said to receive a welcome from the people. Not long before the date of Morse's capture a Catholic priest, arrested on landing, had been sewn up in a bear's skin and 'exposed in the public streets, to be torn in pieces by dogs and sported with as a monster'. In the market-places and shops, wrote a contemporary traveller, 'sacrilegious plunder' was to be had, 'such as chalices, patens, crosses and crucifixes, gold and silver candlesticks, bells, some broken, some sound. . . . The sales were not only public, but announced by leave of the magistrate, with the town crier's bell.'

Morse had a travelling pass, but he was unaware of the sudden and fresh outbreak of persecution during his absence. His own statement is brief. 'Returning to England not long afterwards, the oath of allegiance and supremacy was tendered to me, and for refusing to take it against my conscience, I was thrown into prison.'

The next four years he passed in the New prison in Southwark. Since the scare of the Armada there had never been so many Catholics, clergy and layfolk, in bonds. 'Priests are daily imprisoned,' wrote Fr. Richard Blount, the Jesuit Superior 'many are in danger to starve' if forced to live on their 'allowance of eighteen pence a week.' In one prison nine priests, unable 'to pay as the gaoler exacteth', continues Fr. Blount, were 'all this winter put down to the common prison, without fire, beds or mats to lie on, and with a hundredweight of irons upon them'; from this usage, 'one is already dead, another is dying, and some others be sick'. Outside there was little cause for comfort. Indeed Blount, who can be shown never to have exaggerated, viewed the crisis as the 'most miserable' that Catholics had yet endured. 'Many fall away. Those that stand are ruined in their temporalities.'

All Morse's biographers say no more than that his acceptance of the faith was quickly put to the test—a phrase that covers the four years of his first imprisonment. But there is no doubt that at this time Morse deepened his true Christian sympathy for the physically afflicted which later made him offer his services to the plague-stricken citizens of London. He would have seen something also of the Catholic organisation for the relief of prisoners, which was established in the early years of Elizabeth's reign, and continued its work with the support of collections made throughout the country. On its pattern he may well have modelled the special committee which twenty years later he set up for the relief of the plague-stricken Catholics of London. But nothing is known of these years. Among his fellow-prisoners was the Jesuit Fr. John Falkner, who was chaplain in 1643 at Wardour Castle during its gallant defence by Lady Blanche Arundell and who drew up the terms for its honourable capitulation.

During the whole period of Morse's first imprisonment the persecution continued with intermittent violence throughout the country. In 1616 priests were executed in York, Lancaster, Tyburn and Norwich. But there were lapses also. In April

1618, at the assizes at York, a priest 'was arraigned and condemned, but yielded to take the oath and was reprieved'. A
few days afterwards, on 23 April, Alexander Bucher, who
had been at Douai, and had fallen 'to a dissolute life and
neglect altogether of his function, was hanged at Tyburn with
some of his consorts for coining. The poor man was penitent
for his former life, was reconciled in prison, and died very
well.'

As Morse's last year in prison advanced, the proposal of
Prince Charles's marriage to the Spanish Infanta increased
popular hatred of Catholics, and the pursuivants were made
the heroes of the hour. 'Never had they kept such racket as
now, being set on by puritans to break the match.' At Newcastle-under-Lyme Fr. William Southern was hanged in April.
The following month Blount described the persecution as 'so
extreme that in the north parts Catholics are forced to leave
their houses and live in the woods, to avoid the fury of the
President', and he commented: 'this gives little hope of any
meaning to marry with Spain.'

Spain had set her demands too high—the children of the
marriage were to be educated by their mother as Catholics
and at the same time all the penal laws in England were to be
suspended. However, for reasons of broader policy, James
wished to keep the negotiations open; and he agreed that three
years should elapse before the marriage to ensure that toleration was truly granted. That summer, by way of a gesture, he
sent into exile more than a hundred priests who had been lying
in various prisons. Henry Morse was included in the amnesty.
It seems improbable that he was able to see his family or settle
his estate, for he was in England again, still unordained, three
years later. With his sharp sense of legal justice he resented his
enforced expulsion. 'After that,' and it is all he says of these
four years in prison, 'though not a priest, I was sent into

banishment.' With a large number of priests he was set ashore in France. This was in August. In November, further to propitiate Spain, Sir Walter Raleigh was executed under sentence passed on him for treason in 1603.

3

ROME

Henry Morse reached Douai about 9 August 1618. The Diarist records his arrival and notes that he was known at the College by the name of Ward. Often the student abroad or the priest at home assumed the name of his mother's family, in order to hide his identity from spies who on occasion penetrated Catholic institutions on the Continent. But Henry had been forestalled by his brother William, who was already called Collinson. The three names, Ward, Claxton and Sheppard which Henry later used, may have been a random choice, or, more likely, suggested by family connections.

William, who had completed his course and been ordained priest during Henry's imprisonment, was waiting at Douai to cross to England when his brother arrived with a party of exiles. Throughout August the former prisoners, laymen and priests, continued to gather at the College, and in English fashion the students staged a concert to welcome them; the same month Dr. Kellison, on a visit to Brussels, met Count Gondomar, the Spanish Ambassador to England, who had 'kissed his hand even by force' and had accepted on behalf of the ex-prisoners the thanks which the President proffered for his assistance in securing their release.

The College was now over-crowded. Morse was living out, taking his meals in the College, and paying all his expenses.

As more young exiles found refuge at Douai, it became necessary to despatch a number to the English Colleges in Spain and at Rome. Since Morse was only now beginning his studies, it was convenient that he should be sent. Possibly he asked for Rome in preference to Spain. 'This was his reason for coming to Rome—that as he had received the faith elsewhere, he might absorb it here at its source'—so wrote Fr. Alegambe, his professor of metaphysics at the Roman College.

About the same time that Henry set out for Rome, his brother William left Douai for England. William's departure is recorded for 14 September. In December Henry reached Rome, and sought admission to the English College. He was received there on the 27th by the newly-appointed Rector, Fr. Thomas Fitzherbert. It was agreed that he should be called Claxton, a name by which he was principally known for the rest of his life. He was in his twenty-third year.

As Rector, Fr. Fitzherbert exercised a commanding influence over the community. One of the most outstanding priests of his time, he presented in physique and antecedents a complete contrast to Dr. Kellison of Douai. Born in the last year of Edward VI's reign, he had welcomed Fr. Persons and Fr. Campion to his ancestral home at Swynnerton. He was then a young married man. Seven years later he was widowed and went into voluntary exile, there to practise his religion with freedom. The priesthood was the natural goal of his unworldly life—his daily recitation of the office of Our Blessed Lady and his fasts on the vigils of her feasts. Fittingly he chose the eve of the Annunciation in 1602 for the day of his ordination to the priesthood. During the next ten years he acted as agent in Rome for his fellow secular priests in England: then in 1613 he joined the Society of Jesus. A more suitable choice could hardly have been made for the post of Rector of the English College. Experienced in the mission, as a layman and as a priest, acceptable both to the secular clergy and the Roman ecclesiastics, he was familiar with the courts of France, Spain and Flanders. Deeply spiritual, he was also a distinguished controversialist and theologian; in addition, he was familiar with the ways of the College; as a student he had taken lodgings next to the College and had followed piously in private the routine of the English youths whom he now directed. 'He endeavoured,' says the historian Dodd, 'to render his qualifications useful to all mankind. His purse, his learning, and his interest with men of power, were under that influence. And while he himself declined all preferments, his friends thought him worthy of the purple.' Indeed, 'there was some discourse of that dignity being conferred on him'.

Between the young convert from Norfolk and the aristocratic and saintly Staffordshire Rector an enduring friendship was formed. On his side, Morse, to use his own phrase, was conscious how 'altogether insufficient he was to discharge his duty' of gratitude for the guidance Fitzherbert gave him, whether in winter gatherings round the fire in their common room, or at the spiritual conferences in which the Rector 'expounded some hymn or verse of the psalms and became so suddenly enkindled that tears and sighs would choke his utterance and tremors shake his frail body'.

The course of studies occupied six years. The students now numbered more than fifty. Like other national groups, the Englishmen attended lectures at the Roman College, staffed by an international body of Jesuit professors from all the Provinces of Europe. In their distinctive black cassocks worn loosely over their English doublet and breeches, the students became a familiar sight in the squares and narrow streets of the city, as they made their way to and from their lectures. At home they lived four to six in a room, each with his own desk, table and chair in the centre, and against the wall his bed, made of four planks supported by 'two little trestles', neatly covered by an English quilted mattress. On rising, each student was required to fold his sheets 'handsomely', placing them in the middle of the boards; then he rolled up the mattress and covered it with the quilt. The bell was then rung a second time for half-an-hour's prayer—a practice that Morse and most of his fellow-students maintained to the end of their life. There followed a period of study before Mass. After Mass they passed, still in silence, to breakfast, a quarter of a manchet or fine wheaten loaf washed down with a glass of Roman wine. Lectures occupied most of the morning, the students dividing off to follow the classes in logic or metaphysics, scripture or morals, according to the stage they had reached in their preparation for the priesthood. An earlier generation than Morse's has been trained in religious controversy by Robert Bellarmine, who numbered many Englishmen among his friends and maintained still his ancient interest in the College.

After the morning lectures the students passed their time till dinner in 'walking and talking up and down the gardens'. Two of them in turn were assigned to help the butler and porter serve the principal meal, which consisted of five courses, concluding sometimes with cheeses, sometimes with 'preserved conceits' or figs, or a pomegranate, almonds and raisins. The service was directed by a Brother, who attended also to the repair of boots and clothes, the distribution of linen, and to all the small material needs of the community. 'The dinner done, they recreate themselves for the space of an hour; and then the bell calleth them to their chambers, where they stay awhile, studying the lectures given them in the forenoon. Anon the bell summoneth them to school again, where they stay not past an hour, but they return home again; and so soon as they be come in, they go into the refectory, and there everyone hath his glass of wine, and a quarter of a manchet again, according as they had in the morning. Then they depart to their chambers, from whence at a convenient time they are called to the exercise of disputation, the divines to a Jesuit appointed for them, and every student to a several Jesuit, where they continue for the space of an hour, and afterwards, till supper time, they are at their recreation.'

After supper, in winter time, the students gathered about the fire in a common room talking with the Jesuit community till 'a bell called them to their chamber, the porter going from chamber to chamber lighting a lamp in every one, so when the scholars come they light their lamps, lay down their beds, and go sit at their desks and study a little, till the bell rings when everyone falls on his knees to prayers. Then one of the priests in the chamber beginneth the Latin Litany, all the scholars in the chamber answering him.' And then to bed.

Among Morse's contemporaries at the College were several outstanding men. Some were soon to become his companions in his priestly work in England. Senior to Morse was Fr. Lobb, later appointed classics master to the English boys at St. Omer, where astonished English travellers watched his pupils perform Latin tragedies of his own composition; in his last years he retired to England and there received James Duke of York into the Church. Contemporary with Lobb at the College were Thomas Rogers and John Robinson. Rogers, a Cambridgeshire man, worked for more than thirty years among the poor Catholics of Cumberland, the last mission area assigned to Morse; Robinson for four years was to be Morse's fellow-prisoner, first at Newcastle and then at York, where he had himself been born during the long imprisonment of his father and mother. Two years Morse's junior at the College but twice his age was another Norfolkman, Edmund Downes. In 1637, when Morse lay sick of the plague in London, Downes died of the same infection at Watten, the house of the English

Jesuit novices. Formerly a gentleman landowner, he then divided his time between the management of the estate attached to the novitiate and the spiritual care of the Flemish peasants of the neighbourhood. In attending them during the infection he contracted his sickness and died. Junior again to Downes was Ambrose Corby, who formed a great esteem for Morse and became his first biographer.

During Morse's third year of philosophy, Fr. Alegambe, the professor of metaphysics, not only lectured Morse in that subject but conducted small afternoon classes in which he repeated less formally the subject developed in the morning lecture. 'At the opening of the scholastic year in 1620,' he writes, 'when I had the charge of "repetitions" in metaphysical questions, it was my good fortune, as I look on it, to have Morse as my pupil; and to-day [he was writing after Morse's execution] I have a simple trust that since he belongs to a very grateful nation . . . he may not be unmindful of me.' Alegambe then singles out Morse's earnest and saintly character by way of introducing a tribute that is more than conventional. 'Eminent sincerity' is the first quality he mentions; and then his 'ardent faith . . . so strikingly evident in every sort of student gathering'. The order of the day, Alegambe testifies, Morse observed most carefully; he was 'never missing when there was a domestic task to perform', as, for instance, serving at table, 'and present always at a public one. Each morning he rose promptly, gave due time to study and prayer, attended Mass or, after his ordination, offered Mass at the appointed time.' Although Alegambe suggests that Morse lacked discretion in the physical penances he inflicted on himself—it was only his suspicion— yet it was not these penances that made him remarkable in his professor's notice, but his extraordinary charity. He showed it particularly in the constant inconvenience he suffered in order to place himself at the disposition of English travellers who sought him as guide on their sight-seeing visits to the city. This he did 'time and again'. More interesting is Alegambe's reference to his sudden outbursts of anger. He took his part, says his professor, in the periodic disputes among the College students. 'If there was any dissension among them, as is the way in human affairs, he would defend and follow vigorously the side of his Superiors ... and if he thought he had been rash in his speech and given offence, he was very quick to seek a conciliation, making a humble apology and showing special kindness, although often much senior in age and position to the person he had offended.'

This is more than a conventional statement of humble behaviour. Without direct mention, Alegambe is referring to perhaps the most bitter dispute in the stormy history of the College. Underlying it was an attempt to wreck the seminary. It was instigated by a faction of clergy who used a group of students they had planted there as their agents.

The strife came to a head in 1623, in Morse's last year at the College. He was a senior student and priest, and quickly became the leader of the larger and loyalist section of the students; his name—Henry Claxton—heads the twenty-five signatories in a statement of their case to Gregory XV. The opposing faction, led by Peter Fitton, at its strongest mustered fifteen. Though the strife did not end in the smashing of skulls, it produced threats of this, and each party in turn more than hinted that their opponents were inspired by the devil.

The occasion of the rift was trivial. Fr. Thomas Longeville, one of the senior students, in an outburst of temper had insulted the Rector, and had been sent 'into a chamber apart until his choler should be assuaged, and resolution taken concerning the punishment to be inflicted upon him for his insolency'. At once his friend, Peter Fitton, with deliberate malice, spread a report that Longeville was to be expelled. Fr. Fitzherbert denied that he intended this. Nevertheless, the next day Fitton, failing to get access to the ailing Gregory XV, placed in his secretary's hands a list of charges against the government of the Rector. Immediately his action became known in the College, the remainder of the students organised a counter-petition, expressing their satisfaction with the rule that prevailed and their confidence in Fitzherbert's management of the College. As the main complaint was that the Jesuits in charge were attempting to convert the College into a novitiate of the Society, the quarrel quickly passed to broader issues; rather, it became apparent that it was part of a carefully laid design to wrest the College from Jesuit control.

The Jesuits, it was said, admitted as 'convictores'—that is, students supported on their own funds—young men whom they intended, at the end of their course, to admit into their noviceship. This group, the malcontents urged, were drawn from English families which had always shown 'lavish hospitality' to the Society in England and had many close links with them. It was calculated that in the last five years more than nine students of this class had left the College on ordination to enter the Jesuit novitiate at Liège. The figures were correct. Exception also was taken to the zeal of the Spiritual Father or chaplain of the College—the malcontents now passed from fact to interpretation—in that his annual retreat conferences could only result in the students choosing to a man to join the Society. The Jesuit Fathers, moreover, took advantage of any sickness among the students to persuade them to join the Society—another instance of the way the Fathers 'used' the College 'to get vengeance' on the secular clergy. Indeed, the Jesuits devoted 'to intrigues and plots against the king and country' the time they should have devoted to the students' instruction: consequently when the young priests from the College arrived in England they did not even know how to administer the sacraments. Two capital instances of their political machinations were cited—the veneration paid to Henry Garnet and the esteem of the Fathers for Robert Persons. Under the portrait of Fr. Garnet was inscribed the word 'blessed', and on founder's day, the anniversary of Persons's death, it was the custom to make a speech in his honour. More sinister still, his book on the Succession was to be found in the College library. 'Little better than heretics'—and with their concluding remarks the malcontents came into the open—'the Jesuits, enemies of the secular clergy, as their speech and actions witness, are no fit persons to be entrusted with the training of the clergy'. It was an open avowal of their intention to capture the College for their faction. This done, it might in time become possible to obtain legal toleration for Catholics in England in exchange for the renunciation of all papal claims to jurisdiction, save in the forum of conscience. It was a long struggle, that began before Morse was born and was resolved in principle only in the century following his death. Nor was it the first time that an attempt had been made to get control of the College. On this occasion, working principally through three selected students they came near to achieving their first success. For three months there was nothing but abuse and recriminations to be heard when the students met after their morning classes and, again, after their midday dinner and the evening collation. A settlement was postponed by the death of the Pope in July 1623. In the autumn the new Pope, Urban VIII, advanced the date for the papal visitation of the College, which was shortly due. Six students, including Fitton, were expelled. Longeville, with two other priests, were ordered for penance to say Mass for the peace of the College; another five, to visit the Seven Churches of the city. Ralph Smith, a member of the group, became a Jesuit the following year, not thinking it possible, as he confessed to the Pope, 'to make satisfaction by any other means for the fault he had committed against the Fathers'.

Fitton remained in Rome, and successfully intrigued through the Congregation of Propaganda for a second visitation of the College. It resulted in a decree, forbidding any English student to enter the Society without a special licence from the Holy See. Fitton then left Rome for Douai, where he was ordained priest in September 1625.

It was a stormy ending to Morse's Roman days; nor was it his last encounter with Fitton and Longeville. Five and a half years he had been at the College, with an interval in 1622, when he visited England in order to attend to the settlement of his property, which he had intended to complete before beginning his course.

Before leaving Rome, Morse sought permission from Fr. Mutius Vitelleschi, the General of the Society of Jesus, to join the English Province. He was examined and approved, but owing to the recent decree that he could not be admitted. On 13 July Fr. Vitelleschi wrote to the English Provincial. A fortnight ago, he said, Fr. Morse left Rome; he had earnestly sought admission to the Society, but he was bound by the decree to set out at once for England. If after working there for some time he still wanted to become a Jesuit, then the Provincial was to receive him with great charity and send him to the novitiate of the English Jesuits in Flanders to learn the ways of the Society.

Carrying letters of introduction from his Rector to the papal nuncio at Brussels, Fr. Morse left Rome with Fr. Christopher Warner, Mr. Ward and a first-year student, Mr. Walter Hastings. From Brussels, in an undated letter, he sent Fr. Fitzherbert a brief account of his travels. 'Our journey has been very dangerous. Whereupon we were enforced to take convoys of soldiers, which notwithstanding would scarce have been sufficient, if God had not directed us to leave the ordinary way and so avoid the thieves who attended our coming in the roadway.'

The diversion and the escort strained the financial resources of the party, and Morse observed that the journey had 'been also extraordinarily chargeable, for we paid ordinarily at meals through the Swishers[1] and all Germany five shillings for every one, and for that money could not get a good meal'—indeed for nine consecutive days they were compelled to forgo meat because it was too costly. The religious wars had made desolate the German Palatinate which now looked 'more like a desert than a place inhabited; the land is untilled, the grass groweth until it withereth again'. And Morse continues: 'we saw not a great beast in all the country; the men are very fierce, and as rare there as good men amongst multitudes of secular men'. He was further troubled when 'Mr. Hastings' money failed him', and Morse was compelled to lend his companion three pounds so that he could complete his journey to Liège, where he borrowed a further sum from the English Jesuits in the city. Hastings was an uncongenial companion, and it is clear that there were moments of difficulty on the journey. 'He thinketh our adversaries [the Appellant priests] have the day,' Morse explained, 'and judgeth their cause just'. Furthermore, 'he told me he had much correspondence with them, that he had copies of their proceedings, and that he acquainted Fr. Courtney [a fellow-student] with them'. At Brussels Morse's charity was further tested. He 'was enforced to lend Mr. Ward thirty shillings,' which left him almost penniless, 'in the same predicament with them'. Nevertheless he managed to reach St. Omer where he was given all he needed by the Jesuit Fathers at the College.

[1] Switzerland.

Morse's reason for writing was not, he explains, to entertain Fr. Fitzherbert with his tale of costly and meatless meals but 'to discharge a duty' of gratitude. 'Receive, I pray, gratefully at my hands,' he continues, 'all the humble thanks I can glean you. I do each day entreat Him who is able to remunerate you; and when occasion shall offer itself, I shall endeavour to show myself grateful for such favours that I cannot now requite.' On the evening he wrote this letter, he was ready to continue his journey to the village of Watten, to introduce himself to the Jesuit novice-master—the first indication he gives of his intention to join the Society. 'I think I shall go to Watten this night.' And he adds, 'I hope to remain a week there,' perhaps to make a brief retreat. 'Larger time, you know, is denied me.'

Then hastily Morse closed his letter, 'I am loath to make an end in taking my leave, but I fear to be called away presently; therefore most humbly craving your remembrance of me in your prayers and your blessing,' he signed with his assumed name, Henry Claxton, and prepared to cross to England.

4

ST. ANTHONY'S

WATTEN and the larger town of St. Omer, four miles farther south, lay at almost equal distance from the three ports of Dunkerque, Boulogne and Calais. From Watten Morse could reach the coast at any of these points in a journey of a few hours. Without haste he could embark at night, as soon as a convenient passage might be arranged. He could disguise himself as a Flemish merchant, travelling on business to England, and in this way feign ignorance of his mother tongue, and shun all conversation with his fellow-travellers. Moreover the foreign style of his clothes would cause him no embarrassment. In calm weather the crossing might take as much as two days. From Dover many priests travelled by stage-wagon to Gravesend, and thence up to London by river barge.

It was in London that Fr. Richard Blount, the first and perhaps the most remarkable Jesuit Provincial, had his headquarters. Already his life had been filled with adventures. 'Everyone's favourite', as Robert Catesby had called him, he carried into the new reign the fullness of what was best in the old. He had entered England as a secular priest in 1591 in the canvas breeches and thrum cap of an English tar, under the aegis of a friendly Spanish admiral, magnanimously repatriating a captive taken in Essex's expedition to Cadiz. Lord Howard of Effingham, who examined him on being put ashore, saw nothing to rouse his suspicion. It was his first of many narrow escapes, for the search was always hottest for him. For twenty-one years he was in charge of his fellow-Jesuits—he had entered the Society in 1596—first as Superior of the mission, then as Vice-Provincial and finally as first Provincial. 'My abode at this present', he had written in 1602, 'is and so hath been for some years altogether in London.' Among non-Catholics it was known only to Abbot, the bishop of London, who honoured the secret out of affection formed for him when they were fellow-undergraduates at Oxford. To safeguard his residence which, as his subjects claimed, he was never compelled to change, he kept for the most part at home, accessible only to the rapidly growing number of his priests. Although he received countless letters, yet his identity was concealed even from his servants. To them he appeared an authentic recluse who never left the house. If he had business to do, it was only after they had retired that he emerged late at night, and he was back always before daybreak. Such a figure of legend and mystery did he become that no adjective was too extravagant to describe his apparel. 'If about Bloomsbury or Holborn', wrote the spy Gee in a handbook for priest-hunters, 'thou meet a good smug fellow in a gold-laced suit, a cloak lined through with velvet, with a great store of coin in his purse, rings on his fingers, a watch in his pocket, which he will value above 20 pounds, . . . a stiletto at his side, a man at his heels, . . . take heed': for it is one of the 'prouder sort of priests.' The description was said to apply to Fr. Blount.

The report of his costly and splendid clothes is confirmed by Jesuit sources, which add that at his house, where he received the newly ordained Henry Morse, 'he would be seen in threadbare garments, looking the poor man that he was in spirit'. But the finery was in the tradition of his family, the

Blounts of Blount's Hall, Leicestershire, and he took naturally to it: besides, he needed to be so dressed in the circles in which he moved. Thomas Sackville, Earl of Dorset, Treasurer under both Elizabeth and James, was his convert, received secretly by him into the Church not very long before he died of apoplexy at the Council Table. Already in March 1605 he had secretly visited the Catholic Queen, Anne of Denmark, during her confinement at Greenwich before the birth of Princess Mary. In the remaining fifteen months of her life, Blount 'had occasional opportunities of speaking to her seriously', and reprimanded her for attending her daughter's baptism according to the Protestant form; but it was the Archbishop of Canterbury who had her ear at the end, persuading her against her true conviction to 'renounce the mediation of the saints and rely only on the blood and merits of Our Lord'.

Fr. Blount's discretion and enterprise set the pattern for his priests. In 1598 when Blount took his first vows in the Society in Fr. Garnet's house at Spitalfields, there were fifteen Jesuits at liberty in England, with another four in prison. In 1606, in spite of the disruption that followed the Gunpowder Plot, the numbers had grown to forty-five, and the first English noviceship was established at Louvain. The 'mission' henceforth grew rapidly. In 1614, the year Henry Morse crossed to Douai and was confirmed in the College chapel, there were fifty-nine Jesuits in England and many more training abroad. Five years later the mission was raised to the status of a Vice-Province. For the first time Jesuits in England numbered more than one hundred; rather more were students or engaged in teaching students abroad. Finally, two years before Morse's arrival, Fr. Blount was declared first Provincial. Within another ten years his subjects numbered three hundred and forty-four. This was the full flowering of the pioneer work done by the first generation of English Jesuits.

The work of the Fathers whom Morse now joined had changed little since the time of Garnet. The organisation was also the same, though now more widely extended. For the most part the missionaries were settled singly in country houses or, in larger towns, lodged in taverns and hired apartments. Formerly a single Superior governed the activity of all the Fathers: now each area, embracing usually three to five counties, had its local Superior, as well as an Administrator of the 'College' funds, as the district was called, and a Father whose duty it was to attend to the spiritual well-being of the younger priests. In the next twenty years Henry Morse was to work in three different 'Colleges'.

The months preceding his arrival had been the quietest yet experienced by Catholics. The Court, again anxious for the marriage of Charles, Prince of Wales, to the Infanta of Spain, had given Catholics an unwonted freedom to practise their religion. The Jesuits alone reported two thousand six hundred converts that year. William Bishop, formerly a prisoner at the Gatehouse, now titular Bishop of Chalcedon, toured the country administering confirmation to Catholics for the first time since the accession of Elizabeth. At Holywell, which never ceased to draw pilgrims even in the severest days of persecution, the Catholics became so bold that they entered the public chapel above the shrine and there celebrated Mass. For Fr. Richard Blount the lull occurred at a most welcome time, since he was faced with the need of establishing in England a novitiate for young priests, like Morse, who, fresh from the seminaries, were anxious to join the Society but unable by their College oath to delay as priests on the Continent. By special dispensation from Rome the two-years' noviceship, normally completed in one house, was so adapted for these young Englishmen that only the first year was spent in community, while the second was passed at one of the larger establishments in the country, usually the central residence of the district Superior.

The first house chosen for a novitiate by Fr. Blount was in the village of Edmonton, nine miles north of Bishopsgate. In the Province lists of 1624, the year of its foundation, twenty-four novices are named, including Henry Morse. Only half of them actually lived in the establishment. The rest were scattered throughout the country. Morse himself was immediately sent to the north, to do his first year of training under Fr. Richard Holtby, who, after Fr. Thomas Fitzherbert, was to have the greatest influence in his life.

St. Anthony's, the seat of Mrs. Dorothy Lawson, three miles from Newcastle, on the Northumberland bank of the Tyne, was the centre of the most northern Jesuit district. At Hebburn, close to Mrs. Lawson's establishment, lay the house of her kinsman, Sir Robert Hodgson; across the river, on the Durham bank, at Jarrow, was another Catholic centre organised by John Darell.

Mrs. Lawson, the daughter of Sir Henry Constable of Burton Constable, had been left a widow at the age of thirty-six. The year before Morse's arrival she had abandoned her house at Hebburn to reside at St. Anthony's, a place dedicated in Catholic times to the saint of Padua, whose picture still hung from a tree on the river bank for the veneration of foreign seamen. This new house, built as a Catholic centre, with its chapel, library, secret entrances and hiding-places, was, in the words of her biographer, 'most commodious for pleasure, and pleasant for all commodities; the rich and renowned river Tyne ebbing and flowing in such proportionable distance from the house that neither the water was inconvenient to it nor did it want the convenience of the water'. Under the windows on the south side of the house passed ships from all the northern countries of Europe to take on coal from Newcastle; yet

HENRY MORSE

Newcastle-Upon-Tyne in the Reign of Queen Elizabeth

'Catholics could resort' to St. Anthony's 'with such privacy, that they were not exposed to the aspect of any'. Apart from the neighbouring congregation of one hundred Catholics it served 'sea-faring men of other nations', who came there to fulfil their duties of religion.

Here Morse lived. He served the mistress of the house and its congregation, the miners of Newcastle and the visiting seamen. Here he daily celebrated Mass. On returning at four in the afternoon from his visits to the Catholics of the district, he sang Compline in the chapel, and recited the Litany of Loreto to commend to Our Lady the 'safety of the house, and a *De Profundis* for the faithful departed'. After dinner, between eight and nine, the Fathers recited the Litanies of the Saints, 'at which all the servants attended'. On feast days they gave a catechetical instruction. This Mrs. Lawson, with all her neighbours' and servants' children never missed, for she 'delighted to hear them examined and to distribute medals and *Agnus Deis* to those that answered best'.

The eve of Christmas 1624 was spent in prayer. After the customary Litanies of the Saints at eight, there were confessions and an instructional sermon. Then Mrs. Lawson and her Chaplain remained in prayer till midnight, when the three Christmas Masses were said, 'which being ended all broke their fast with a Christmas pie and departed to their own houses'.

On this day, her biographer tells us, Mrs. Lawson 'unbent the stiffness of her bow a little, and dispensed with her accustomed rigour. . . . For whereas at other times she never played at any game for money, but for prayers, for an hour after dinner or supper at Christmas she allowed herself every day two hours after each meal a shilling to spend among her friends to make them merry. . . . If she won she kept her earnings in a purse to bestow after her holidays on the poor, over and beside her accustomed alms.'

Fr. Richard Holtby, the founder of the Jesuit stations north of the Humber, lived for the most part at St. Anthony's. His was already a great name among Catholics when, in 1581, Edmund Campion visited the north-east under his protection. So discreetly did they ride together across the moors from house to house that it is impossible even now to trace their journey during the weeks they were together; indeed there is a total gap for this period in the records of the Government that succeeded in tracking down Campion's hosts in every other part of the country. This is remarkable, for the danger was greater in the northern parts of the kingdom, where as John Gerard observed, 'many of the common people are Catholic and almost all lean to the Catholic faith'. Here conversion by small communities was possible, although 'they easily scatter when the storm of persecution draws near and return again when the alarm has blown over'. And Gerard might have added, that while the prisons of London and the south were filled for the most part with gentlefolk, it was the artisans, labourers and yeomen who crowded York and other northern gaols. The old feudalism was stronger. Houses like Mrs. Lawson's at St. Anthony's and Sir Robert Hodgson's at Hebburn were but rarely disturbed.

Born at Fraiton in Yorkshire in 1553, Holtby was in his seventy-second year when he received the young novice from the English College in Rome. Like Morse, he was a graduate of Cambridge. Ordained at Cambrai in 1578, he crossed to England the following year. Shortly after Campion's martyrdom he had ridden south to seek admission to the Society. Failing to find the Jesuit Superior, Fr. Jasper Heywood, in London, he went to the Continent, and was appointed Superior of the newly founded Scots College at Pont-à-Mousson. In 1589 he was back in England, and till his death in May 1640 at the age of eighty-seven he was stationed permanently in the north. From southern Yorkshire to the Scottish border he was, in Gerard's phrase, the 'father of all the Churches'.

A little man with a reddish beard, he was an accomplished mechanic, carpenter and stone-mason. At St. Anthony's and in all the stations he established he constructed hiding-places with such skill that none was ever discovered by the pursuivants. The vestments at St. Anthony's were his work, for he was skilled also with the needle. Unlike Morse, he enjoyed robust health, and until the day of his death, five years before Morse's execution, he never suffered a single day's illness. While Morse was imprisoned five times, Holtby eluded capture all his priestly life.

Most of the stations which Morse visited had been founded by Holtby. Few of them can now be traced, for Holtby directed the movements of Morse and his other subjects with such discretion that no Mass-place of his was raided in this period. Gateshead was perhaps the earliest of all, a Catholic residence on the site of the medieval hospital of St. Edmund and the Holy Trinity, which had passed into the hands of the Lawsons at the time of its dissolution. To the south of it, two stations were established on the Wear, at Durham and at Harber near Plasworth. Stella House, a seat of the Tempest family two miles up the Tyne from Newcastle, was another ancient centre. Places farther north are difficult to date with certainty; but Berrington Hall, Haggerston near Berwick, and Callaly Castle, which flourished later in the century, may date from Morse's time.

Fr. Morse's arrival coincided with an alarm at the increase of Papists in and about Newcastle. From Appleby Castle, on 10 September 1624, Lord Clifford, the Lord Lieutenant, had written to the Council confessing that in Northumberland the Papists were 'so powerful and so adhered to by the thieves that His Majesty cannot find one man in ten to do him service',

while among the gentlemen they formed such a 'faction' that
if those 'firm in religion were not encouraged, his Majesty's
best servants will come to the worse'. It was a fear springing
from unknown strength and the memory of a Catholic rising.
The plague was raging, and Newcastle 'so infected, so ill-
fortified, so ill-neighboured' or surrounded by Catholics that
Lord Clifford reckoned that five hundred men could ransack
it. Holtby, concerned only with his flock, continued his
priestly work. As Rector of the Scots College he had taken
care of the plague-stricken townspeople of Pont-à-Mousson;
and now he initiated Fr. Morse into a work of charity that was
to make his name famous in the Catholic community.

It is easy to reconstruct Morse's activity during the months
of infection, and to see him at dusk making his way on foot up
the road that passed north of St. Anthony's to the Pilgrim's
Gate of Newcastle, the finest of the seven gates that broke the
circuit of the massive walls, strengthened against the Scots by a
rampart within and by a ditch on the outer side. Before the
road passed under the gate the priest saluted Our Lady at her
famous shrine of Jesmond or Jesu de Munde, to which, the
chronicler tells us, came pilgrims 'from all parts of the land in
time of superstition'.

Within the walls Newcastle was still a fair city in spite of its
industrial prosperity. A century earlier it claimed forty religious houses; still it possessed four fine parish churches. St.
Nicholas, the greatest of them, stood dominating the river
Tyne, a long and noble church, with a stately stone steeple and
lantern tower resting on four arches, the work of Robert de
Rhodes, the Lord Prior of Tynemouth in the days of Henry
VI. It was the pride of the burghers, who saw it 'lift up a head
of majesty, as high above the rest as a cypress tree above low
shrubs'.

It was on the east side, lying towards St. Anthony's, that lay the most populous suburbs, where Henry Morse would best be known to the growing section of the people who obtained their livelihood from coal. Here also, outside Sandgate, lived the shipwrights, seamen and keelmen, their dwellings dwarfed by the high and broad bridge of five arches that connected the town with Gateshead on the Durham bank. With its old chapel and cluster of shops and dwellings it was more picturesque than Deanbridge within the town or Stockbridge at Pampeden below it. The steep banks of the river, lined on the north side with long wharfs, allowed ships to lie safe from storms and, with the help of two large cranes, unload their cargoes of wine or corn or discharge their ballast in all seasons. As the export of coal, particularly to London, increased, more ships carried ballast than wares. While the menfolk cut coal, the poorer women of the town unloaded rubble, carrying it in baskets to Ballast-hill, east of Sandgate. 'It was the best ballast shore out of town, since which time, the trade of coals increasing, there were many ballast-shores, made below the water on both sides of the river.'

It was a period of speculation and poverty. Apart from the local magnates, who employed as many as a thousand men, gentlemen from the south had hazarded large fortunes in the pits. The enterprise of Mr. Beaumont was much discussed among Morse's Catholic flock. A man of 'ingenuity and rare parts', he had ventured into Newcastle with thirty thousand pounds and rare engines unknown to local mine-owners. Although he introduced boring rods of iron and others for testing the depth of the coal, to say nothing of wagons with one horse, and machines for drawing water out of the pits, yet 'within a few years he consumed all his money and rode homeward upon a light horse'. The misadventure of such southerners provoked cynicism rather than hostility among the natives. 'When they come to crack their nuts,' it was said of rich Londoners, 'they find nothing but a shell . . . meteors, *ignis fatuus*, instead of a mine.'

More assured of a livelihood was the population employed in the west part of the town known as the 'Glass Houses'. Here was manufactured plain glass for windows and exported to all parts of the kingdom 'to the great profit of the town'. Like the salt production on the Durham bank, the manufacture of glass required less capital than coal: indeed, the salt pans of Durham were famous for their white salt, boiled with New-castle coals. It was an industry that was ideally situated; and less lucrative only than the production of grindstones from the river-bed, which again were so widely distributed throughout Europe that there was a proverb, indicating the people's con-tempt for their traditional enemy, which promised a traveller that 'a Scot, a rat and a Newcastle grindstone you may find all over the world'.

On the Wednesday of Holy Week 1625 Fr. Morse was home at St. Anthony's for the full liturgical ceremonies traditional before the Reformation. On the evening of Wed-nesday and on the two following evenings, Tenebrae was sung, 'with the mysterious candlestick of fifteen lights, fourteen of them representing, by the extinguishing, the apostles and disciples when they left Christ, the fifteenth, on top, His dear mother, who . . . from the crib to the cross was not severed from Him'. And the biographer continues, 'On Thursday, a sepulchre, decked with sumptuous jewels, was reverently attended day and night by her family and neighbours . . . and on Saturday she caused to be extinguished every fire in the house and kindled again with hallowed fire. Then ensued the benediction of the Paschal Candle, and the rest of the divine ceremonies till Mass. At Mass, as soon as the priest pronounced *Gloria in excelsis*, a cloth was suddenly snatched away which veiled a glorious altar, and many little bells, prepared for the

purpose, rung in imitation of what is done with greater cere-
mony in Catholic countries.' The climax came on Easter
Sunday, when Mass was followed by the blessing of 'divers
sorts of meat', including always a portion of lamb. 'Finally
those that repaired there that day for their Easter communion
which were sometimes nigh a hundred, were all invited,
according to our phrase, to "break Lent's neck" with her, in
honour of Christ's joyful and glorious resurrection.'

The Easter celebrations this year were followed by a
revival of persecution, which, as always, fell more severely on
the north of England than the south. The negotiations for the
Spanish marriage had broken down; there was no further need
to woo Spain with half-hearted promises of toleration. France
provided Prince Charles's bride, who as Queen Consort was
to prove more than once Morse's friend and protector. The
aldermen of Newcastle feigned alarm, and claimed to fear a
papal assault from the Catholics settled without the walls; from
the Lawsons at St. Anthony's, Sir Thomas Blackstone's at
Petteworth, Sir John Claxton and Mr. Swinburne's at Cap-
heaton. But the town, ordered to fit, victual and furnish with
ordnance a hundred ships for the King's service, preferred to
re-enforce the fines against recusants than exact a levy from its
burghers. It was a method also that helped to calm the fears of
the ecclesiastical authorities, for by reducing the resources of
the Catholics, it was thought to render them incapable of an
armed rising. About the time Henry Morse was celebrating
Easter with Mrs. Lawson, Thomas Fuller, in his *Appeal of
Injured Innocence*, published that year, proclaimed his alarm at
'the activity of the Romish priests to gain proselytes and their
dexterous sinisterity in seducing souls'. He feared that if
Catholics were given the toleration promised them in the event
of a Spanish marriage, 'the plausibility of Popery to vulgar
judgments' and its 'lasciviousness . . . to the palate of flesh and

blood' would prove irresistible. He admitted 'the negligence of too many ministers in feeding their flocks' was matched only by 'the fickleness of our English nation' to embrace what, with an historical lapse, he described as 'novelties'. It was a confusion of fear backed by a monetary interest, but it served to inspire the persecution that impeded Fr. Morse's last months of work in Durham and finally led to his arrest.

The rejoicings in October 1624 when Charles returned without the Infanta augured ill for Catholics. From the time of Babington's conspiracy they had learned to be apprehensive when the populace set out in the streets tables loaded with wine and sack. Soon after Easter 1625 it was known that Charles I had married Henrietta Maria by proxy in Paris. She arrived in London in June. Later that summer the plague broke out in London. In the autumn the expedition to Cadiz returned in costly disgrace. All was set for the renewal of persecution. In December writs were issued for the enforcement of the laws against recusancy, a promise which had been wrung from Charles in his first Parliament. As the meeting of Parliament grew near in January 1626 proclamations were issued against the Papists.

5

THE SEA HORSE

IN the north-east the pursuivants were more numerous and remorseless than in any other district apart possibly from London. Durham and York were the two northern hubs of their activity. On an instruction sent out from the Council in Westminster it was possible to set quickly in motion a widespread organisation for 'hunting down and harassing' the Catholic community. It was Morse's fate to pass his missionary years in the very centre of the enemy's network. Other less conspicuous or more fortunate priests might have evaded capture; but Morse's chances were small, for he soon became notorious for his universal charity.

The term 'pursuivant' was used to designate any person who by office or self-appointment made or supplemented his livelihood by exacting the statutory reward for the arrest of priests. It included also servants of the sheriffs and the ecclesiastical authorities. In an attempt at classification, a Catholic writer, possibly Fr. Holtby himself, reckoned that 'of the pursuivants there are twelve kinds'. The servants of the Privy Council or King's messengers came first, followed by the officials of the 'pseudo-bishops'. These were peculiar to the north and went about 'two and two', citing Catholics each month before the ecclesiastical courts where the oath of allegiance or supremacy was tendered to them. The expenses of this class were born by their victims themselves at the rate of 'thirteen pence per mile', for they had no other occupation and were 'unceasingly engaged in searching'. The remaining ten groups illustrated varying kinds of personal enterprise in pursuing Catholics: from individuals with private bands of hired ruffians to limited companies whose members shared the profits of the pursuit. It was such a company, perhaps the longest established, with branches both in London and in the north, that was for twenty-four months to shadow Morse at night through the streets of London. Equally dangerous, because better informed, were individual apostate priests. In Durham and Yorkshire William Johnson, during Morse's brief sojourn there, was the most notorious of this group and betrayed to the Governor of York Castle all the old hiding-places in a number of northern houses where he had been received as a missionary. Nor was there any redress in law against the informer. Large Catholic establishments such as St. Anthony's were in some measure protected by the number of their own retainers: but, as Fr. Morse went from station to station ministering to the poorer Catholics of his 'College', he would have heard many tales of terror. In his district there had been a destitute woman; she had nothing left in her cottage to buy off a persistent bailiff, apart from a length of cloth which she had concealed to serve her as a winding-sheet on her death. This was seized and she was then carried off to prison.

Morse's first arrest as a priest was due to a mischance.

On the morning of Friday, 31 March 1626, John Johnson Hart, Master of the *Flying Hart*, a collier based on Calais, made his way on the midday tide past North Shields up the river Tyne. On board he carried four passengers, Anthony Van-denhaupt, a Fleming from Mechlin, a middle-aged Englishman and two young English boys returning from school abroad. In the early afternoon, midway between Shields and Newcastle, the ship anchored close to the south shore off the point called Hankebill, opposite St. Anthony's on the Northumbrian bank. The passengers disembarked. Anthony carried with him a trunk belonging to Mr. Thomas Fairfax, whom formerly he had served for three years as valet during his Continental tour. He had also a 'cloak-bag' containing his personal belongings, and a large case, described as a 'fardel', which the ship's master, John Johnson Hart, refused to release. There had been a misunderstanding over the payment of the passage. John Johnson Hart claimed that Vandenhaupt had promised him four pounds for the passage for all four persons. This Vandenhaupt denied. He protested that he had contracted merely for himself. It was agreed therefore that the fardel should be held until the full passage money, which Anthony did not carry in his purse, should be delivered.

In the ship's boat the four passengers were taken to the house of John Dann, a servant of Mrs. Lawson's neighbour, Sir Robert Hodgson, on the south bank. There they lodged the night. The next day Anthony Vandenhaupt crossed to St. Anthony's and thence continued his journey by road to Newcastle, there to recover his fardel from the *Flying Hart*. The chief customs officer, William Swan, was aboard. The fardel had been seized. In dismay Anthony 'struck his breast' and exclaimed in the hearing of the captain 'that it had been as good for him to have been hanged'. He was arrested at once and lodged in Newcastle gaol.

The fardel had aroused the searchers' suspicions. It was addressed to Mr. North, the name which Fr. Holtby sometimes assumed. That in itself was unrevealing, but the contents were manifestly contraband—more than eighty-two books destined for the priests' library at St. Anthony's: Aquinas, Ambrose, four volumes of Cyprian, the works of Cardinal Cajetan, Thomas of Lyra, handbooks for confessors and preachers, tomes of reference for canonists, a concordance to the Bible, devotional and liturgical books and a special Missal printed abroad *pro sacerdotibus Itinerantibus in Anglia*—the nucleus for a library of the kind that Fr. Blount was trying to provide for the principal house of each district, useful to a retired missionary who might spend his last years in devotional writing or controversy. Besides books there were 'beads and relics of Popery' in the fardel, with letters and instructions addressed to several English priests. Anthony Vandenhaupt disclaimed knowledge of the contents or acquaintance with Mr. North, and unsuccessfully tried to place the ownership on his travelling companions who were now safely in hiding. Indeed his story was not improbable. He said that five years previously he had entertained at Brussels Mr. Thomas Fairfax, son of Sir Thomas Fairfax of Gilling, and had been taken into his service, returning with him to Walton in Yorkshire after three years on the Continent. There he had fallen sick for the space of a year, and rejoined his master, who in the meantime had taken up his residence at St. Anthony's. From Thomas Fairfax he transferred his services to Sir Robert Hodgson at Hebburn and was with him until Mr. Ralph Cole, sheriff of Newcastle, commissioned him to obtain the release of a Gateshead mariner, Robert Young, from Dunkerque, where the man had been imprisoned after a skirmish at sea. It was from this assignment, apparently unaccomplished, that he was now returning. Nevertheless he was imprisoned.

On Wednesday, 5 April, after examination by the Mayor and aldermen of Newcastle, John Johnson Hart was allowed to take on coals and prepare for the return voyage to Dunkerque. At the same time, at a neighbouring wharf, another collier, the *Sea Horse*, likewise registered at Calais, was making ready for the same voyage—an English vessel under an English master, with an English crew. On Wednesday, 12 April, she weighed anchor. As she sailed down the Tyne, intending to put to sea on the early afternoon tide, her master was hailed from the north bank by a man and a young boy. It was an arranged signal. The ship's boat was lowered and the two passengers were taken aboard.

Fr. Morse had recently returned from a visit to the southern section of the district. The previous Saturday he had arrived at Durham, stayed there the week-end that Anthony Vandenhaupt had visited Newcastle to claim his fardel, then went on to Chester-le-Street, where he took a room at an inn on the Tuesday night. The next morning he sold his horse and continued his journey on foot to Hankebill. There at Dann's house he met by arrangement a young lad, John Berry, who had been a pupil of Mr. Conyers at York, and was now on his way to Douai to finish his education at the school recently started by Dr. Kellison. Without delaying, Morse and Berry crossed to the north bank. There they hailed William Carew as he passed downstream in the *Sea Horse*.

Henry Morse had been in England about eighteen months. He was still a Jesuit novice, under obedience to Fr. Holtby. He had not yet taken his first vows; nor had he made the *Spiritual Exercises* for thirty days, a part of the novices' training never omitted, no matter how much else was adapted to the needs of the mission. From his later movements, it would seem that Fr. Blount was anxious to send him to Watten in Flanders to live in community there rather than in the Edmonton house, where living was dangerous on account of the plague. Waiting at Calais to return in the *Sea Horse* was Fr. John Robinson, who had been appointed to succeed him at St. Anthony's.

John Dann knew the fate of Anthony Vandenhaupt, but he was confident that he could arrange an unmolested passage for Morse and John Berry in another vessel. On the previous Saturday, while the *Sea Horse* was loading coals at Newcastle, he had called on the ship's master, William Carew, and agreed on forty shillings for their passage to France. Warned by Anthony Vandenhaupt's misfortune, the two travellers carried little baggage: 'each of them a pie, two loaves of bread, one cheese, a cloakbag and a few eggs'; and as soon as they had stepped on board, William Carew made them change their dress for mariner's clothes so that they might, as Morse later explained, 'pass unknown'.

Unhappily rumour of their passage had reached William Swan, the customs officer at Newcastle. Possibly there was mention of it in the letters captured on Anthony Vandenhaupt. As the *Sea Horse* followed the channel, about forty yards broad, that passed to the north of the shelf of sand at the river mouth and led close under the commanding guns of Tyne-mouth Castle, William Carew was ordered to cast anchor. A boat put out from the bank, bringing Dudley Swan, brother of William Swan, of Newcastle. Suspecting, as he stated, 'the man and the boy to be seminaries', Swan ordered them ashore and held them prisoners in his house while he summoned William to conduct the examination. Meanwhile Morse played the part of a foreign gentleman returning to the Continent from business in Newcastle. At first 'he would speak no English but all Italian'. William Swan arrived. For another two hours Morse sustained the pretence. He used also some Spanish and French, but he was unconvincing. Then he changed his bluff. He frankly declared himself an Englishman, and gave his name as Thomas Sheppard. Then he tried to bribe the searchers. William Swan was adamant. Finally he simply begged 'their favour to pass', but with no success. The two officers pointed out that his release would bring them into jeopardy with the higher officials of the port. But Morse was ready with his reply. 'You may set two men to watch me,' he suggested, 'and when they are asleep I will slip away.' Thus he could 'pass without prejudice to themselves'. The suggestion was not considered. The *Sea Horse* continued its way, and the search of Morse's person began. In his pocket was found a pair of beads 'with a picture of brass', as Dudley Swan described it, 'at the end'. This was his rosary with the crucifix attached, for in travelling it was perilous for a priest to be found with a breviary, and it was customary to substitute the beads for the divine office. His purse contained exactly four pounds fifteen shillings in gold and other coins, just sufficient for his passage and his journey overland to Watten. And for the rest nothing was found save three sheets 'written on every paper, but what the words [presumably Latin] were, Dudley Swan could not tell'. The final question put suggested that his passage had been stayed on information found on Anthony Vandenhaupt—had he been at Hebburn or did he know the place? He denied that he had even heard the place mentioned.

The report of the preliminary examination, endorsed 'information concerning he that is suspected to be a priest and the boy', was despatched to Newcastle. The following day, Thursday, 13 April, Fr. Morse was twice brought before Thomas Liddel, the mayor, and five aldermen for further questioning. In the first part of the report there is mention of Broome, Cambridge, and Barnard's Inn, and a statement of his movements carefully presented to conceal his studies in Rome and his recent work at St. Anthony's. The final question he could not evade. Had he received the Anglican sacrament twice last year, as by law bound? To this Morse refused to answer on oath. The bluff was over and he recognised it. Firmly he admitted he was a Roman Catholic and said he hoped so to die. The oath of allegiance was proffered. He rejected it.

In his second examination the same day, Morse successfully

parried the attempt of the board to wrest from him a confession of his priesthood. Was he a Jesuit, a 'seminary' priest?
Rather than equivocate, for technically he might claim that he
was neither, but a priest awaiting admission into the Society,
he chose to attack. What right had the Mayor to demand on
oath an answer to the question? The statute 'did not require
him' to reply. That was true: Morse was more cognisant of
the law on this matter than his examiners. His statement was
accepted. The Mayor continued. What did he hold concerning the deposing power of the Pope? Yes, Morse admitted that
the Pope had such power: it was the common teaching of theologians that the Pope could depose princes, but only 'for some
just cause, if they deserve it'. The beads and relics were his
own, given to him by friends in England. Finally he was asked
to declare on oath that 'all his answers were without equivoca-
tion or mental restriction', but here the examiners had exceeded
their rights. 'There is no authority', he retorted, 'by any
statute whatsoever to require me to answer on oath.' He had
failed to secure his release, but he had foiled his examiners. In
a last attempt to convict him of receiving Orders from beyond
the seas, a barber from Newcastle, Edward Bambrigg, was
brought into court. True, he had not seen him at the altar, but
'twice or three times last summer', Bambrigg testified, Fr.
Morse called 'at his master's shop to have his hair trimmed'.
On the first occasion he was in company with Mr. Henry
Lawson of Broughton, and at another time with Mr.
Thomas Fairfax. He had called last about three weeks before
Christmas.

Such evidence increased suspicion, but proved nothing.
From the court Morse was taken to Newgate prison. He never
stood his trial, nor was his priesthood proved against him. He
might well have been released through the influence of Sir
Robert Hodgson, had not another incident increased the

Mayor's alarm and determined him to seek the instructions of the Council in London.

Seventeen days after Morse had been imprisoned, a collier, the *Fortune*, registered at Enkhuizen in Holland and sailing under an English master, Yorkin Johnson, passed North Shields and anchored at Newcastle. It was Sunday, 30 April. William Swan had been informed as soon as she entered the river. Before the passengers could be disembarked he had boarded the vessel. There he discovered a Dutchman, a Scotsman and a boy. While Swan's men held them in custody, a search revealed 'divers letters written to Englishmen, together with many books, pictures and faculties of priests'. At once the letters and other 'portable' things were sealed and sent to the Council. The ship's master was held for examination, along with Zachary Vanderstyn, the Dutchman—he could speak no English, but only Dutch and French—William Steward, the Scotsman, and the boy, Thomas Berry, whose home was at Kirby Knowle in Yorkshire and who was no relation of John Berry of Jarrow, who had been arrested with Henry Morse. On the following Monday all four made their appearance before the Mayor and the same group of aldermen who had examined Henry Morse.

William Steward was a Scotsman, from Stratherne, a *bona fide* traveller returning from a three-years' sojourn in Paris, where he had sought a health cure. His portmanteau, sword and apparel were no evidence against him, and though 'inclined to Catholicism than otherwise', was ready to go to church and take the oath of allegiance. There was nothing to disprove his story and he was allowed to continue his journey after taking the oath. Thomas Berry's history was less uncompromising. Unlike Steward, who had arrived at Calais the day before the *Fortune* sailed, the boy had lodged for ten days at Calais in the same inn with Zachary Vanderstyn while the master saw to certain repairs and was further delayed by cross-winds. He carried beads on his person. He had been discovered hiding from the searchers when they boarded the vessel at Newcastle; he possessed no pass; and finally he refused the oath of allegiance. He admitted he was a Catholic.

The presence of a Catholic boy escorted by a foreigner, who professed himself a Catholic and claimed to speak no English, presented a similar pattern to the recent discovery made on board the *Sea Horse*. When a chest, containing a further consignment of theological books, was found on board, Zachary Vanderstyn stood little chance to bluff the examiners. Moreover, the steersman and others of the crew believed he was a Jesuit; they had heard him speak English to his fellow-passengers during the crossing. But in spite of this testimony, Zachary Vanderstyn refused to admit that he knew the language. He was a Dutchman, he insisted, born at Damm in Brabant. No, he was 'no Englishman and no Scotsman, but the countryman he said he was'. His emphasis grew. There were two reasons why he had made the journey: first, for his health, since 'the season of the year was fair'; then, to recover a debt from a fellow Dutchman resident in Newcastle, Mr. Francis Vandersteggin. He hoped to find his debtor through another Dutch friend, Vanderswain, to whom he had letters of introduction—Vanderstyn seeking out Vandersteggin through the good offices of Vanderswain. His invention of Dutch names aroused suspicion. Although they could not prove it, the examiners, from letters already in their hands, suspected his true identity—Fr. John Robinson, a fellow-student with Morse in Rome and a Jesuit now for six years under the assumed name of John Taylor. The books, he declared, had been brought over for a Frenchman whom he did not know personally. He had been instructed to leave the chest on board until it was collected by the man's servant, doubtless John Dann. In his pocket he had little more cash than Fr. Morse, two gold pieces of twenty-two shillings each, and two or three silver coins. He refused the oath. He had been a Catholic, he said, all his life—that was true enough, for his parents had long suffered for the faith in York Castle—and he explained that in his native land of Brabant 'there are both Catholics and heretics'.

On the evening of 1 May 1626 Zachary Vanderstyn *alias* John Robinson joined Henry Morse in Newgate gaol overlooking the wharfs where William Swan maintained his watch for contraband fardels and 'seminaries' masquerading as Dutch traders.

Minutes of the examinations had been posted to London, and Richard Neile, Bishop of Durham, a tireless correspondent of Secretary Conway on matters of coastal defence, fortification and fisheries, organised a search of all the Catholic houses on both the north and south banks of the Tyne. Within six weeks he reported that 'several raids' had been made. On each occasion Sir Robert Hodgson was absent from his Hebburn residence; there was no trace of John Berry at Jarrow or of his neighbour, John Dann, at Hankebill. The arrest of Anthony Vandenhaupt, now in Durham gaol, followed within a month by the capture of two suspected priests, had exposed a dangerous network of Catholic families co-operating in illicit smuggling of books and priests. The constant absence of these suspects, the bishop reluctantly explained, made further 'examination or security of their persons' impossible. The most he could now do was to emphasise how 'very dangerously near the river' they dwelt 'for the receiving and conveying of popish passengers and their carriage of what kind soever'. All the recusants, 'reputed pragmatical in offices', should either be removed from their habitations or ordered to some other place, away from the river, which gave them 'less opportunity for their evil endeavours'. His zeal was not unrewarded. In the following year he was appointed to the Privy Council and shortly afterwards transferred to Winchester. John Dann returned to Hankebill and continued to serve as Dorothy Lawson's trusted smuggler.

6

YORK GAOL

ERECTED on the site of the ancient Berwick Gate in 1390, Newgate was the most strongly guarded point in the town's defence works. In 1399, when Newcastle was made a separate county, two wings were added to provide a common gaol for the prisoners, who had previously been housed in the castle. It had now fallen into disrepair, 'so weak', the authorities complained, 'that many escape from it, and so noisome and infectious that many prisoners die'.

Fr. Morse, whose health was never certain—in the descriptive list of the Province at this period his physical condition is described as mediocre—was saved the fate of many inmates by the kind offices of Mrs. Lawson. 'Preferring their conveniency before her own safety,' she visited him in Newgate, 'furnished him with Church stuff,' so that he could offer Mass, 'washed his linen, and provided him with all necessities for clothes and victuals', and, moreover, arranged with the magistrates that he should 'enjoy the liberty of the town for his health'. The gaol however was small, and to make room for more criminals, Morse and Robinson were shortly transferred to York Castle.

After Newcastle and Durham, the gaol at York was of worse repute than any in England. Built by William I to overawe the people of the north, it was later used as a fortress against the

Scots. From the beginning of the fifteenth century it had been
allowed to decay. In 1478 Richard III converted it into a
gaol—for it was an age of open warfare and castles such as
York were, as Camden remarked, 'only fit for those who want
courage to face an enemy in the field'. Its keeper, Samuel
Hales, had been granted the office in February 1617 for a period
of sixty years. It was an office of quick profit, and its holder
sold the post of assistants at whatever price he could command
—at York the price was high, for the castle was never empty of
Catholic prisoners. The men Hales attracted were no different
from the Newgate gaolers; at best 'worn-out soldiers', but 'for
the most part the very off-scum of the rascal multitude, cab-
bage-carriers, decoys, bum-bailiffs, disgraced pursuivants,
botchers, chandlers and . . . their stinkardly companions'. A
predecessor of Hales, in the previous reign, had introduced a
new scale of charges for York prison, including an entrance
fee for Catholics, who were always put in irons when they
passed into his custody. 'At their first committing and entry
every Catholic yeoman pays ten shillings for fetters, every
gentleman twenty shillings, every esquire forty. . . . Among
gentlemen', the writer explains, 'they number priests, though
in other usage they esteem them for the worst.' Although their
priesthood had not been proved against them, both Morse
and Robinson were graded as 'gentlemen'. But it was a matter
only of expenses, for in other points Hales did not respect the
differences laid down by his predecessor. Without distinction
of birth or social position, Catholics fared ill, by comparison
with the most forlorn inmates—'cattle-thieves, coin-clippers,
murderers, common cut-purses, and all sorts of malefactors'.
They at least had some slight protection in law; but the Catholic prisoners had no redress against the extortions of their
keeper.

Intolerance in the north-east of England was frenzied. The

number of Catholics that died in York Castle and in the Hull blockhouse is unrecorded, but the deaths were constant and numerous. Herded together, men and women indiscriminately, in cells without light or ventilation, they were a prey to every plague, and when the river flooded, died from fever in rooms which were partly under water. For the meanest fare they were forced to pay the most exorbitant prices, for no purchase could be made except from the keeper. Often they had 'nothing to subsist withal but the charity of well-disposed persons'. Nor were they permitted to benefit fully from the kindness of friends, since they could not 'buy a bit of bread or a drop of drink, nor so much as a halfpennyworth of milk' or a little firewood in the winter except through the keeper, paying him 'twopence or threepence for that which is sometimes not worth a penny'. Even the peaceful practice of their own devotions was denied them. On Sunday, frequently, they were taken forcibly to the Minster to listen to Protestant preachers. Occasionally the magistrates brought up from the south a special proselytiser for the purpose, and among others, Edmund Bunney, a broad-faced, bulky and self-styled apostle, so 'fluid' in his grim harangues that his reluctant Catholic listeners complained that 'he was troubled with the divinity squirt'. In the absence of other priests, Morse and Robinson organised what relief they could. The task was difficult, for while they collected alms and administered the sacraments, they had to keep their priesthood secret from the gaolers. Nevertheless, as Fr. Alegambe states, 'their success was almost beyond belief, such generous offerings did they receive and distribute among the needy Catholics. They cared for them with great self-sacrifice, giving them food to keep them alive and the spiritual comfort of the sacraments as well. Both priests celebrated Mass daily.'

After each Assize condemned criminals were led out from

the castle to be hanged at the York Tyburn outside Micklegate Bar. Less than a year after Morse had been transferred from Newcastle, William Cawan, with his accomplice Bill Hall, was executed there on the morning of 30 March 1627. Their offence had been housebreaking at Halifax, aggravated by the attempted murder of John Williamson, his wife Ellen and their two little children. Whatever help the Fathers could give these men, they gave them; but Robert Storie, just over a year later, would receive no spiritual comfort: on 2 April 1628 he died 'very hardly, in the presence of eight or nine thousand people'. But the day came when the ministrations of Fr. Morse were more than blessed. A man and his wife were lying in chains in the inner dungeon where criminals were lodged the night before their execution. Immediately above, in a large cell shared with other Catholics, lay Morse and Robinson. Throughout the night the oaths of the two sinners 'filled the whole place'. Robinson could do nothing—his only hope of release lay in sustaining his impersonation of a Dutch trader from Damm. He spoke to Morse in Italian, as he always did in the presence of non-Catholics. He urged him 'to caution the criminals on the pains of Hell; then to instruct them both in the faith. This done, he was to ask them whether, if a priest were present, they would wish to be absolved.' Thus advised, Morse entered their dungeon; he silenced their oaths, and with a gentleness that never failed to win the most degraded men, he passed the night teaching them the principles of the faith. Before daybreak they expressed a wish for absolution, if it could be given. Without revealing that he was a priest, Morse silently and without their knowledge absolved them.

The next day the townspeople turned out in thousands to watch the executions. The gossip along the road and in the alehouses was all of previous executions—of William Cawan, Robert Storie, and William Borwick, whose jest to the hang-

man made the crowd think less unkindly of him for murdering
his wife. He trusted that the rope was strong enough, he said,
because if it broke and he fell to the ground, he would be
crippled for the rest of his time. This was the great moment in
the criminal's career and in his last seconds of life he was supported by the consciousness of his celebrity. Would the next
man die with a gesture of bravado or defiance, or how would
he seek to make his death memorable in the city's annals?

Morse's converts of a few hours surprised the city. Something special might be expected from the joint hanging of
husband and wife. Instead, 'they died devoutly these good
thieves, professing themselves openly to be Catholics'. Their
behaviour roused Protestant York. At the next Assizes a
clamour was made against the suspected interference of the two
priests lying still in gaol. But the judge dismissed the angry
petitioners. 'Whatever they thought of the matter,' he said,
'and whoever it was who instructed them, there can be no
question that they were well instructed. This was the couple
that the other day had vowed vengeance on me and I don't
know who else. When they came to die they were praying to
God for us all.' There the matter rested. But quietly and still
secretly Henry Morse continued his prison apostolate, and so
effectively, writes Fr. Alegambe, that 'it is worth noting how
all the time Fr. Henry was in prison, practically every criminal,
before being led out to execution, was brought by his gentle
endeavour into the Catholic Church'.

From outside the prison, either in person or by messenger
from St. Anthony's, Fr. Holtby continued his care of his
former subject. He appointed Fr. Robinson his novice-
master, and under the guidance of his cell-companion, six years
his senior in the Society, Fr. Morse made the *Spiritual Exercises*
for thirty days. On St. Ignatius's meditations—so simple and
fundamental—Morse spent the greater part of his day. The

solitude was absolute. His vocation had already been tested in the streets of Newcastle and among the poor of Durham. It was a deepening of his purpose that he experienced, not any difficulty in choice of life: that had been made. Delicately Fr. Alegambe explains that though Fr. Robinson was wise in matters of the spirit, it was 'the Holy Ghost, the teacher of men's hearts', that directed Morse. 'The place', he adds, 'where the priest prayed in seclusion from the crowd was closed to the light of day; thus the Holy Spirit worked more familiarly in his soul and gave more deep instruction to his heart. It became his daily trade, his single concern, to attend first to his own salvation and perfection and then, as opportunity later offered, to that of his neighbour too.' The pattern of his life was set, his purpose strengthened; for the rest, he advanced imperceptibly to its achievement in singleness of intent. Ambrose Corby, who was his contemporary at Rome and his constant friend, could say of him that he 'truly walked before God, that he might be perfect, and everywhere showed himself a good servant of Christ, and to many a saviour of life unto life, always most observant of discipline, a lover of the Cross of Christ and of labours, upright and sincere in mind, full of zeal, and fuller still of piety'.

At the close of his retreat, in his first year in prison, Fr. Morse resumed his charitable works in the prison, aiding Catholic and non-Catholic alike. Three years later he was released. The exact date is unknown. It was probably during the March Assizes, 1630. Though not proven a priest, he was exiled. The sentence was for life: but for every priest it was considered a formality. Sentenced to exile or not, they were, in any case, outlawed by the country to which they devoted their comfortless lives.

It was probably at the same Assizes in York that Fr. Robinson was condemned to be hanged, drawn and quartered outside Micklegate. The sentence was not carried out, but he lay in York Castle for another eleven years, providing for the relief of Catholic prisoners. No longer in need of disguise, he ministered openly to the condemned malefactors. As an old man he told of his days as novice-master in gaol and the story of John Bartendale, the felon whom he had confessed on the eve of his execution on 27 March 1634. Bartendale had been a strolling piper. After he had hung on the gallows three-quarters of an hour he was cut down for dead and buried near the place of execution. The hangman had not reckoned on the strength of Bartendale's throat muscles. Shortly afterwards, Sir Thomas Vavasour of Haslewood, passing on his way to the city, saw the freshly-turned soil heave close to his path. At once he dismounted, and with his servant's help, 'dug up the convict all alive'. At the next Assizes the Judge mercifully ruled that Bartendale was legally dead. He was released through the intercession of his deliverer, who took him into service at Haslewood: but in intervals of work he went into town,

> And in York continued blowing
> Yet a sense of goodness showing.

7

FLANDERS

In the seventeenth century Watten was a fair-sized town, lying back twenty miles from the coast. There, in the early summer of 1630 Morse arrived on being landed without fardel or cloak-bag from the English ship that took him into exile. The novitiate of the English Jesuits, removed from Liège, was finely situated on a hill behind the town, looking out to the Channel on the north, and to the roof-tops of St. Omer to the south. The building was a dismantled monastery, formerly the property of Canons Regular. The dilapidations had been made good, and on 8 September 1624, shortly before Morse had passed through on his way from Rome to England, the first High Mass had been sung in the old Church, with organ and choir, and with a solemnity that had not been seen since its first foundation by the Canons. Already it had proved a most suitable house for training the young Englishmen in the ideals of the Jesuit life. Although it was more than four years since Morse first sought admission to the Society, he had not yet lived the routine life of prayer and work that was the pattern of the novitiate. 'Exchanging prison for exile', writes Alegambe, 'he crossed again to Belgium and for some time lived the life of the novices at Watten, giving a singular example to his companions.' Shortly afterwards he was appointed to priestly work.

Situated on the borders of the Spanish Provinces of the Netherlands, the town at this time served as a base for the Spanish army defending the frontier towns. In the month of Morse's arrival on the Continent, a peace treaty had been signed in Madrid between England and Spain. Without tension of loyalties the English priests at Watten were free now to minister to the Irish and English soldiers attached to the Spanish forces. In September 1629 Frederick Henry, Prince of Orange, had taken Hertogenbosch on the Brabant border and in the next twelve months defeated the dispirited and ill-paid Spaniards in a series of engagements.

The number of English mercenaries was now increased and each year, when the troops went into winter quarters in the neighbourhood, the Fathers at Watten arranged special services for them at their Church. In the campaigning season two or sometimes three English priests lived with the troops in the field. It was to this work that Morse was assigned in the autumn of 1630. 'That winter', says Fr. Alegambe, 'the English troops were billeted in the hamlets and villages around Watten,' and Morse in all weathers sought them out, catechising them in the faith, giving courses in controversy, ministering the sacraments of the Church. He was indefatigable. Before the fighting season started in the spring, he had fallen sick. 'He had strained himself to the limit of his endurance', Alegambe continues, 'watching at the bedside of the sick, journeying from billet to billet, visiting the injured in improvised military hospitals—his care of his flock was *extra modum*,' more than his body, weakened by imprisonment, could sustain. Near Cassel he collapsed—he realised he was critically ill. The Flemish Fathers there received him into their College, expecting that he would die. But his power of recovery, as he was to prove again in the next ten years, astonished his brethren. 'With constant and devoted nursing he recovered his physical strength.' Ambrose Corby says the same: 'it was the extraordinary care and kindness of the Flemish Fathers,' and particularly of the Rector, Fr. van Middelen, that saved him. The community prayed for him daily, invoking St. Francis Xavier, who was held in great honour in the College, for the Fathers there, only three years before, had been given a relic of the saint.

In May fighting was resumed. Morse was considered fit only for convalescence. His duties in the field were taken over by another priest from the novitiate. As soon as he was strong enough for work, he was appointed to the post of Minister of the house.

It was now Morse's task to provide for all the temporal needs of the community at Watten, and at the same time to take care of their health, no slight responsibility in a foreign country where young Englishmen—there were thirty-four novices this year—frequently fell sick with strange fevers. He was responsible also for the discipline of the house and for the services in the Church.

Ambrose Corby stresses the care Morse had of the sick. As he wrote, he would have recalled Morse's concern for his own father, an old blind Brother in the Watten community. After Brother Corby's three sons—Ambrose, Morse's friend, Ralph, his fellow-martyr, and Robert—had joined the Society, and his two daughters, Mary and Catherine, had taken the veil as Benedictine nuns in Brussels, he himself at the age of seventy had entered the novitiate. He lived another nine years and had the final comfort of receiving his own father, a Protestant, into the Church in his one hundred and first year. Doing odd jobs that Fr. Morse gave him, he passed his days united to God in prayer.

Morse's attention to the sick is mentioned also by Alegambe, who writes further of the harmony in which he worked with the Rector, Fr. Henry Bedingfeld, and with the Procurator, Fr. Edmund Downes. Both, like Morse, were Norfolkmen belonging to families familiar to John Gerard. Downes had been Morse's fellow-student at the Roman College. Now he shared with Morse the temporal administration of the house; he also managed the modest estate, and in his spare time assisted, as Morse did, the small band of missioners who attended to the spiritual needs of the native population.

This work was considerable. Flemish came with difficulty to the tongue of the English priests. But each Sunday Morse went out to preach and hear confessions in the neighbouring churches. The novices, too, as soon as they had sufficient vocabulary, visited more than fifteen parishes, the remoter ones on horseback, to teach the elements of religion to the village children, who listened with pleasure to the young Englishmen speaking their language.

At Watten the church of the Jesuits had already become the principal Catholic centre of the district. As at Liège, St. Omer and Ghent, the English Fathers attached to the student houses entered without reserve into the life and interests of the people who had welcomed them to their country. Two or three times a year the Flemish clergy of the diocese of St. Omer gathered at Watten to make the *Exercises* under the direction of an English priest. It was a novel practice, and no less startling than the frequency with which the natives, under the guidance of the English priests, came to Holy Communion each month —several hundred often on feast days from a distance of six or seven miles. During Lent of 1632 a course of special sermons was arranged. It was an innovation; and at first all but a few seats were empty, for 'the labouring people, tired after the week's toil, either stayed idle at home or, worse, squandered their wages in the taverns'. The special preacher, in spite of the efforts of the catechists, addressed an almost empty church.

Then, as a device to draw the people, Morse rehearsed the local children in a Passion Play. Under his supervision the sanctuary was converted into a stage. At intervals between the discourses, the story of the Passion was enacted. 'The tender age of the children, their clever acting, the changing stage-sets, and the novel form of instruction, succeeded as none of the Fathers had hoped. The audience was often stirred to tears, and the church, large as it was, proved too small to hold the crowds.' As news of the plays spread in the countryside, 'multitudes flocked to the Church, the inns were deserted and in despair the keepers themselves came to the *Exercises*'.

Before the close of 1633 Henry Morse was transferred to the English house in Liège, to hold there the same office of Minister. It was the customary and prudent measure of the Provincial to occupy abroad for an interval of a few years any Father who had been formally exiled from England. For the most part these were marked men and ran greater danger of arrest if they returned while their first arraignment and imprisonment was a recent occurrence. Possibly also, it was judged that Morse, who had overtaxed his health, was still too weak for the more arduous life of the mission. For another twelve months he remained abroad.

The house at Liège, founded in 1614 as a novitiate, was now used by the Jesuit students of philosophy and theology. With the assistance of his English friends, John Gerard had purchased for his building one of the finest sites within the city walls, nearly twenty acres, stretching from the confines of the citadel down the steep slope of the northern ramparts to the edge of the residential quarter of the city. Gerard's first building consisted of two blocks erected at the base of the property, which ran with a narrow street—later called the *rue des Jésuites Anglais*—leading to the Hôtel de Ville and the ancient Cathedral of the Prince Bishop. In 1624, when the novices were removed to Watten, another wing was added, containing a chapel, lecture halls and common rooms. On the first floor lived the Rector and eight professors; and above, in the smaller rooms, the student Jesuits. It was a larger community than at Watten; there were forty-two studying philosophy, twenty-four theology—figures that indicated a still-growing English Province. With the Fathers teaching and others engaged in controversial writing and in other works, the English community without passing visitors numbered ninety-two. After St. Omer and Douai, it was the largest English settlement outside Rome. The Rector, Fr. Francis Wallis, had been Morse's fellow-prisoner in the New prison, a saintly man from Surrey, whose capable tenure of office left little for the historian to record.

The life of the English students was passed in pleasing surroundings. From the house the gardens rose in finely planned terraces to the highest part of the city. There, remote from the noises of trafficking in the market below, they climbed to read and study in summer-houses built to an English pattern drawn out in rough by Fr. Gerard. Beneath lay the unadorned but not unattractive College buildings: on the hill to the west the fortress-like Church of St. Martin; to the south, across the island in the Meuse where the rich merchants had their houses, and beyond the meaner dwellings on the farther bank, rose the foothills of the Ardennes. Liège was not yet the armoury of German city-states, but still a proud and beautiful city, fierce in its independence and hospitable beyond expectation to the English community that sought asylum from its ruler. The courage of the Englishmen combined with their unostentatious devotion appealed to the citizens. The English Jesuits, distinctly but perhaps unjustly preferred to their native brethren, were invited to lecture in the University. Fr. Edward Leedes, better known as Courtney, took the students of the first year in logic and general metaphysics and gave lectures there in controversy, during the intervals of writing. He was the convert son of Sir Thomas Leedes, K.B., and had already engaged Windebank in debate over the oath of allegiance. After Morse's death he was appointed Provincial. More brilliant and original than Leedes was Fr. Francis Line. Among the leading scientists of his time, he was occupied that year erecting in the College garden his own type of pyramidal sundial. Charles II, who saw it when he visited the College on his way to Spa, later brought him over to construct a more elaborate model in Whitehall. It was a composite structure, which, in addition to the hours, expressed by the sun's shadow many facts or fancies of geography, astrology and astronomy. Besides several works, including his classical *Treatise on the Barometer*, he wrote vigorously against the young Isaac Newton's theory of the refraction of light. Finding by experiment that the sun's image, when the sky was clear, was round and not oblong, he ascribed the elongation noticed by Newton to the effect of clouds. Irritated by the challenge, Newton did not deign to reply for many years. It was only in 1675, when old Fr. Line lay dying at Liège, that Newton's letter reached him, acknowledging his miscalculation.

Across the river, about a mile downstream, a path ran from the bank up the steep slope of the first hills of the Ardennes. About half a mile from the summit the Liège community had their small and simply furnished summer residence, *La ferme des Anglais*, as it was then known. Its upkeep was the responsibility of Fr. Morse, and each Thursday the students left the city for a day there in the country. A small but typically English park sloped from the front of the house, leaving a far view over the city to the west, and to the east down the wooded Meuse in the direction of Namur. On either side of the house lay orchards, and beyond, in the woodlands, a shrine to Our

Lady of England, where Morse prayed for the end of his exile. Later, a decade after Morse's departure, it was discovered and adopted by the people of Liège. They built a chapel to house the Madonna, and later still, transferred her to a neighbouring hill where they constructed the basilica that now towers over the city with its unsightly and massive dome.

Even more than at Watten, the Church of the English Jesuits was thronged by the townspeople. They liked the orderliness of the services rendered by the English. 'Great crowds flocked to the Church,' a report says, 'which was not big enough to hold them, and more than once the Church doors were broken in by the pressure of the multitudes.' There was also the regular instruction of young English converts, about twelve each year, undertaken by the Fathers. But the work, varied and fruitful, was an unsatisfying substitute for the English mission. The air of Liège had benefited Morse's health. In 1633 his chance came. Fr. Blount had undertaken to send Fathers to Maryland to accompany the first Catholic settlers On 22 November, with the cognisance of the Provincial, Fr. Andrew White secretly boarded the *Ark*, anchored at Ryde in the Isle of Wight, and, landing in southern Maryland, became the father and founder of the Church in the King's American colonies. To replace him in London Fr. Blount drafted Morse back to England. 'He was overjoyed.' Before the close of 1633 he had left Liège. This time he was appointed to the London district.

8

ST. GILES-IN-THE-FIELDS

In his first letter after his arrival, Fr. Andrew White, a Londoner by birth, contrasted the broad flowing Potomac, 'the sweetest and greatest river I have ever seen', with his native Thames, which 'is but a finger to it. There are no marshes or swamps about it, but solid firm ground, with great variety of wood not choked up with undershrubs, but commonly so far distant from each other as a coach and four horses may travel without molestation.'

Nevertheless, to the foreign traveller London also, which Fr. White had exchanged for Indian settlements, was a fair city. Its inhabitants had long claimed that it was 'glorious and ancient', and considered that if only 'the brick and timber buildings could be rendered stone and marble it might become another Rome. It commands the proud ocean to the Indies and reacheth the furthest Antipodes.' But since its fires were stacked with Newcastle coals, its 'stately head', complained John Evelyn, had become 'wrapped in clouds of smoke and sulphur, full of stink and darkness'. The streets were very 'narrow and incommodious in the very centre and busiest places of intercourse'; the cobbles underfoot 'ill and uneasy'; the passage-ways and alleys a labyrinth unravelled except by their inhabitants, while overhead the spouts and gutters provided 'a continual wet day' after every storm. The constabulary was inadequate, the numerous bye-laws intermittently enforced. In time of plague it fell victim almost overnight, and the authorities could do nothing but allow the visitation to run its course.

The nuisance of soot and smoke was worse in St. Giles, where Morse was set to work, than in any suburban or city parish. It was not so much the cooking fires that caused it—their fumes were 'hardly discernible', and in any case, were 'scattered above'—but the furnaces below the street level, belonging to brewers, dyers, lime-burners and boilers of soap and salt. An observer reckoned that a single furnace in St. Giles infected the air more than all the chimneys of London put together. Through vents and tunnels at street level they were 'constantly belching forth from their sooty jaws', so that it made the poor but newly built parish appear already ancient, 'more like a suburb of hell than the imperial seat of our incomparable monarch. For when in all other places', a contemporary writer complained, 'the air is most serene and pure, the sun itself is here eclipsed with such a cloud of sulphur that it is hardly able to penetrate; and the weary traveller, at many miles distant, sooner smells than sees the city to which he repairs.'

At night, when Morse went round the Catholic tenements, the furnaces were low, but there were other disorders. Immodestly clothed women, 'generally reputed for notorious common and professed whores', sat or stood in the doorways of victualling houses, or in other 'base tenements, exposing and offering themselves to passengers'. An order of the Middlesex County Court in 1626 did nothing to curb the nuisance. Although stocks were set up that year for 'night-walkers' at the expense of the Earl of Southampton, the Lord of the Leet Court, 'the honest sort of inhabitants' continued to protest. Intermittently throughout the next ten years officers and constables were ordered to return lists of all landlords 'who enter-

tain, harbour or suffer to abide in their houses such lewd,
dissolute and defamed women', but the abuse persisted. Only
an occasional prosecution would be made, when whoring led
to violence or murder.

In daytime the soot-soiled streets were no pedestrians' paradise. It was only ten years after Fr. Morse's death, in the time
of the Protector, that the authorities, acting on a surveyors'
report, attempted to enforce bye-laws making for orderliness.
There was still no method of compelling the householder to
rake the filth in front of his own door. Refuse, offal, carrion
and ashes could be tipped without penalty into the street by
housewives impatient of the arrival of the raker's truck.
Brewers and water-carriers, in overloaded carts, tore up the
cobbles with their spiked wheels; even swine were suffered to
wander up the lanes. The Earl of Southampton drew his rents.
He had already paid for the parish stocks; the cost of repaving
the streets was later divided between him and the parish.

From the time of Cardinal Allen the city, the largest of the
kingdom, was always the surest refuge of priests. There, in
apothecaries' shops and in taverns, where strangers passed in
and out during night and day, they were unnoticed and un-
marked. They tended to take lodgings in the more densely
inhabited streets, in Holborn, Bloomsbury and St. Giles-in-
the-Fields, still on the northern fringe of the city, and in Shoreditch, Whitechapel and Wapping in the east. These boroughs
gave quick access to open country in time of search, or to the
woods, Epping Forest to the east, St. John's Wood to the
north; they contained also the worst slums and the largest
grouping of the Catholic population in the country, many
hundreds of poorer craftsmen, butchers, bargemen and
hostlers, as tenacious of the faith as the shepherds of the Lan-
cashire fells.

It was principally in the parish of St. Giles-in-the-Fields that

Morse worked for the next four years. During the first decade
of Elizabeth's reign it had been a secluded village; earlier still
it was remote enough from the city to be chosen for the site
of the gallows at the junction of the High Street and Oxford
Road when Smithfield was considered too populous for
regular public executions. But as the village grew, the gallows
was planted further west at Tyburn. Still, however, in memory
of its former distinction, the sheriff's procession halted a few
minutes outside St. Giles's church, while the criminals were
given a large goblet of ale—the famous St. Giles's bowl—as
their last refreshment this side of eternity. The people remembered that at this place, two hundred years earlier, Sir John
Oldcastle had been burnt to death. It was a memory that may
have accounted for some of its bitterness against Catholics
and the still recurrent fears that they would rise up and seize
the city by violence. Loose words spoken in wrath were
reported to magistrates. Open praise of Rome or priests on the
lips of innocent old ladies could be taken in law as incitement
to rebellion. Not infrequently there were cases like that of
Elizabeth Shipley. Calling non-Catholics 'heretical dogs', she
claimed that though on any day she herself and many of her
friends might be 'gone out of town, yet there were Papists
enough left to hang all the Protestants and Puritans'.

The Catholics of St. Giles were conscious of their strength;
nor were they confined to a single class. Indeed, the wealthier
sort was prosecuted less frequently for non-attendance at
church, but this was because they lived partly in some country
residence. In London their stone-built houses in the more
fashionable streets and the new squares provided convenient
'massing-places', more secure against the incursions of spies
than the upper rooms of taverns. Occasionally three or
more priests gathered to sing the full ritual of High Mass; and
once, when a householder like Henry Good and his wife

Anne—they lived in Queen's Street—were indicted, the jury
returned a verdict of not guilty. Magistrates were now dis-
inclined to convict unless their hand was forced. For the most
part they left Catholics to practise their religion in precarious
freedom. Often they tolerated worse offences. For instance,
Mr. James Looker of St. Giles was one of several Catholics
who maintained a small teaching establishment, taking in boys
till they were old enough to pass overseas to Douai or St.
Omer.

Nevertheless, it was only in the Queen's chapel at Somerset
House that Catholics were permitted to worship openly. And
'they never entered it or left it but in a crowd; and while some
were within attending the august sacrifice, others were waiting
at the door'. Each day 'there was a continual ebb and flow of
people from six in the morning until twelve at noon'. And the
writer, a French Capuchin who served the Queen, himself saw
the King watch them from a window of the palace, 'by his
silence approving of their devotion' and seeming 'to condemn
the unjust laws of the Parliament against the Catholics, who in
fact are his most faithful and best subjects'.

The number of secular priests in London and in the outlying
villages is not known. Probably they outnumbered the Jesuits,
who in the year of Fr. Morse's arrival had only thirty-one
priests in London. Fr. Blount was still Provincial; his Assistant, or Vice-Provincial, was Fr. Matthew Wilson, more widely
known in learned Anglican circles as Mr. Edward Knott. He
had been a prisoner in the Clink, and now he lived 'about the
Custom House'; here between visits to Lord Falkland's house
at Great Tew, he wrote his controversial books, balanced in
cumbrous phrasing 'within the mean, betwixt uncharitable bitterness and pernicious flattery' on the subject of the salvation
of Protestants. William Chillingworth was his convert and
later, after a brief sojourn in the Society, his antagonist in this

extended debate. Always in poor health, but tireless in his attentions to his subjects, he now received Morse for work in his district shortly after completing his treatise, *Charity Mistaken*, in reply to *Want of Charity* by Christopher Potter, the Provost of Queen's.

Like other areas, the London district was organised as though it were a regular Jesuit residence such as the house at Liège. The Minister of the 'College' was Fr. Philip Fisher, who, soon after Morse's arrival, sailed to Virginia to refound the Church there. Fr. Edward Lusher, a fellow Norfolkman, who had crossed from Flanders at the same time as Morse, became his closest companion in London.

Plots and pamphlets sustained the animus of the people against the Catholics. On 25 November 1633, within a few weeks of Morse's arrival, an unfortunate Irish Dominican from Westmeath had been arrested and arraigned. He was reported to have declared that he would kill Charles I, if only he could get at him, because he was a heretic. At Tyburn he was cut into four parts which, contrary to custom, were not displayed on the four gates, but instead carried abroad to be respectfully buried by his friends. Recurrent incidents of this kind made credible the persistent propaganda that Catholics were regicides, a race that 'kill princes, sow sedition, blind the simple, abuse the honest, bereave the innocent, swear and foreswear'. There was always a section of the London populace ready to believe anything heinous of their Catholic neighbours, convinced that they themselves imbibed 'the pure water of life' while the adherents of the old faith 'waddled in loathsome puddles . . . kissing their babies and kneeling to wooden ladies'. Tales of the Gunpowder Treason were kept alive. The thirty English Jesuits working in London were represented as a secret regiment of four orders waiting and working for the chance to overturn the realm. The first 'order' was made up of 'ecclesiastics, the second of politicians, the third of seculars, the last, the intelligencers or spies, men of an inferior sort', who insinuated themselves into the service of great men, so ubiquitously that gentlemen were cautioned 'lest they entertain a Jesuit or Romish spy in their houses instead of a servant'. With the kingdom nourishing so many orders of Jesuits, it was readily believed that 'all Spain, France and Italy' could not 'yield so great a multitude of Jesuits as London alone'. Thus, in the heart of the realm, their chief plotters had imported a special 'India-nut stuffed with the most sharp poison' which was kept 'prepared for the King's assassination'. The routine triennial meetings held by the Fathers with the object of selecting representatives for the customary Congregation of the Society in Rome were distorted by pamphleteers into weekly assemblies more sinister than any Titus Oates revealed in the reign of the King's son. At the Angel tavern in Long Acre the Jesuits were said to have their headquarters. There 'the intelligencers assemble and confer in common what thing everyone of them has finished that week'. With members of the first order, the ecclesiastics 'or conjured members of the Society', they assembled there, arriving 'frequently in coaches or on horseback in layman's habit and with great train, that they may not be known'. Other secret gatherings known only to a few of their members were reported in more fashionable quarters. The whole of Queen's Street was rumoured to be their property. Here a 'Jesuitical College was tacitly built', and outside the city at Greenwich, the Countess of Arundel, a 'strenuous she-champion of the Popish religion', had established a convent of nuns, where girls were educated before being sent 'hither and thither into foreign monasteries beyond the seas'.

Underlying all these rumours was a fragmentary substance of fact, furnished by the small group of clergy who kept constant touch with Protestant leaders. Peter Fitton, Fr. Morse's antagonist at the Roman College, was now the clergy agent in Rome. In October, in the year of Morse's arrival, Fitton received from England a letter from Fr. Benedict Norton, which leaves no doubt concerning the intention of the chapter of the secular clergy, controlled by this faction since its establishment in 1624. In their own words, their aim was to 'animate' the laity to deliver a petition to the King 'for the banishment of the Jesuits as incendiaries and disturbers of the public peace': this would be enough 'to send them all packing hence'. And with this object they spread abroad worse calumnies against Fr. John Gerard, now chaplain at the English College, than the Council had ever ventured to fabricate. The story was circulated in print that in 1605 Gerard, toiling in a sweat shirt, had helped to dig the mine beneath Parliament while Guy Fawkes prepared his barrels of gunpowder.

Morse would have appreciated the odious irony of the situation—Fitton, receiving as official agent of the clergy, a letter in which the venerable Gerard was made a lever for the expulsion of his brethren from England. 'And although they think', the writer continued, 'that they have friends at the stern, yet I am confident they have none such as durst appear in public to cross the signing of such a petition. But suppose they had, the petition . . . would not be long from being put into execution, it lying always in a readiness for the State to make use of; and in this his Majesty would be cleared to the whole world from all touch of persecution, since it is done at the earnest petition of his own Catholic subjects.' Had it not been 'for the general neglect of our most just cause' in Rome, continued the writer, he would have long since pointed out in Latin letters 'to his Holiness and to the Holy Congregation' of Propaganda the 'desperate' damage done to the Catholic cause by Fr. Blount's machinations.

Now, assigned to work in St. Giles, Morse found his fellow-Jesuits and the secular priests at odds with the mischief-making chapter. Seldom able to conceal his vexation, he was angered often and strong-spoken. Deputed on the outbreak of the plague to work with John Southworth, the chosen representative of the chapter, he quarrelled with a violence that he regretted when he came to die.

9

PRIEST OF THE PLAGUE

In the early summer of 1635 the plague was reported on the Continent. In August, when it struck Dunkerque, causing great loss of life, Sir Robert Parkhurst, the Lord Mayor of London, wrote in alarm to the Council. He proposed a proclamation to prohibit all vessels from Flemish and French ports landing persons or goods without licence, and, furthermore, urged a period of quarantine for all travellers coming ashore from the infected places. But it was not until the 3rd October that these precautions were taken. The same day an Order in Council set watchers on all incoming ships to prevent the landing of goods or persons until the lapse of twenty days. For the most part the order was enforced, but occasionally the cordon was broken by an insistent traveller like Baron de la Ferté who obtained horses at Great Yarmouth and rode with his retinue to Court within two days of landing. Rightly the plague was considered infectious; and experience of previous visitations had made the London authorities fearful of ships from foreign ports.

In May the plague had reached its peak in Flanders and Germany. On the twenty-fourth of this month the Earl of Arundel, the newly appointed Ambassador to the Court of Vienna, reached Cologne—the first city he had entered that was free of the plague: indeed, they had passed some towns where they were uncertain whether 'the very house they have lain in had been free'. Between Cologne and Frankfurt they found 'scarce any people left', so that the Earl was forced to carry his provisions with him. From Nuremburg, on 19 May, his secretary told how 'one night they came to a village, which they had wholly to themselves, for there was not one living creature left in it . . . the country was all spoiled and depopulated'; dying people to whom they offered bread were 'so far finished that they were past eating'. The plague, following on the ravages of war, had left the country a desert.

It was not until late in the autumn that the first case of plague was reported in London, in the parish of St. Giles-in-the-Fields. It was nothing unusual. Londoners had been familiar with the carbuncles and sores—the plague spots—that had marked the infected for centuries. There was no alarm among the people.

Although it lay without the city boundary, St. Giles was essentially a town area. Its streets were a byword for squalor. Overcrowded in any case, the ill-shaped wooden tenements had already become the chosen refuge for the destitute scourings of other parishes. Throughout the winter a few cases of plague deaths were reported each week: but the infection at this stage was hardly distinguishable from typhus, which was endemic in the London slums. Slowly, however, the plague followed the circuit of the walls, striking the outlying parishes of St. Olave's, St. Mary's, Whitechapel and St. Sepulchre-without-Newgate, and the straggling district of Stepney, stretching from Shoreditch to Blackwall. Here in twisting alleyways lodgers, herded together in conditions of filth, were defenceless against contagion.

In the winter months, before the outbreak was recognised as more than a minor recurrence, Fr. Morse continued his customary round of priestly duties. It was only in April, with the coming of the warmer weather, that the plague began to take an alarming weekly toll. Then London endured all the rigours of a plague-stricken city. The regulations of 1625, the year of the last plague, were re-enforced by an Order in Council dated 27 April. Justices of the peace were now empowered to cause 'every house wherein lies anyone who has been visited with the plague, to be shut up and watched by day and night'. Special plague inspectors or 'searchers' were sworn in, with watchers, buriers, and bearers, each with his settled wage. The taking-in of lodgers was forbidden all householders; a special tax for the relief of the stricken was levied on each parish, and the justices empowered to construct pest-houses or timbered huts where the victims could be segregated.

It was now that the Catholic community in London was forced to organise its own measures of relief. Since no Catholic name appeared on the parish registers, they were excluded from official help. So far they had survived, like the rest, on the charity of friends.

At the end of April, after the publication of the plague orders, the Superior of the London Jesuits, Fr. Matthew Wilson, met the chapter of the secular clergy. It was agreed that the Society and the seculars should each appoint a representative who would devote himself solely to the plague-stricken Catholics, and administer to them whatever funds could be set aside for their relief. The choice of the secular clergy was Fr. John Southworth, several years senior to Morse, and already a veteran missionary, and member of the chapter. Fr. Wilson selected Morse. The reason for the appointment can only be guessed. Fr. Southworth, as events proved, was no easy man to work with. Morse had known him at Douai, and perhaps the friendship formed at that time had been strengthened by association in London. Moreover, Wilson had heard of Morse's work in Newcastle, during the visitation of 1625;

possibly also, in the rigorous restriction on movement and visiting imposed by the parish authorities, he considered it wise to appoint a priest who was familiar with the law and could work in understanding with the magistrates.

There is no indication that Morse volunteered for the work. Alegambe suggests the contrary. 'When Fr. Henry', he writes, 'heard that he was appointed to the task, he went about in high spirits, unable, it appeared, to restrain himself. No better news, he said, could have been given him. He was chosen for that work—and he hoped that through his means many souls of the dying would be snatched for heaven.' Ordinarily reserved, he would seem from the moment of his appointment to have made no secret of his happiness.

Morse's friends, who knew that his health was uncertain, might have questioned the wisdom of Fr. Wilson's choice. However, throughout the preceding winter Morse had been working without interruption. From the annual reports of the London Jesuits it is clear that for many months now all the Fathers in the infected areas had been nursing the plague victims. 'The visitation gave them an opportunity to show true charity, and they were quick to take it.' All through the winter, 'they were called upon to administer relief, bodily and spiritual, to the poor Catholics'. It was only in April, when the plague began to spread alarmingly, that it became necessary to provide more than haphazard relief.

On the instructions of Fr. Wilson, Morse prepared for his work by retiring for a week to the Jesuit house at Cheam, a pleasant Surrey village rather more than an hour's ride from the Strand. Here in a small rest-house belonging to the Fathers, he made his annual retreat. The gardens and the country surroundings made it a most suitable refuge, where each year the Fathers could withdraw for a brief period to make the *Spiritual Exercises* and, as Fr. William Weston wrote,

TO THE
CATHOLICKES
OF ENGLAND.

RIGHT HONORABLE, RIGHT WORSHIPFVLL, AND MVCH RESPECTED:

VVE vnderwritten being appointed to serue the infected Catholicks of the Citty and Suburbs of London, with our spiritual assistance, hauing seene with our eyes the extreme necessity which many of the poorer sort are fallen into, by reason of the present sicknesse, do thinke our selues obliged euen in conscience, to make the same knowne vnto you, by a publicke letter, to the end that those, whom God hath ble'st with sufficient ability and meanes, taking so weighty a matter into their serious consideration, may, through the help of his holy grace, resolue with themselues forthwith, to doe what in them lieth, and what in such an exigent Christian charity and duy bindeth euery one vnto, for the necessary support and reliefe of so great a multitude.

Wee doe protest vnto you seriously, euen vpon our soules and consciences, that the greatnesse of this calamitie exceedeth all beliefe, in so much as wee should neuer haue imagined the least part, of that which really is, had not our owne eyes, and daily experience sufficiently attested the same vnto vs, and wee may truly auerre, that this so great a desolation amongst our poore brethren, ioyned with the small meanes and power wee haue, to relieue them, is a farre more grieuous affliction vnto vs, then all the labours and dangers, which wee vndergoe daily for their spirituall ayde and comfort.

There are some persons in the number of these afflicted, who, notwithstanding they were well borne, and bred, hauing beene constrained, through extremity of want, to sell, or pawne all they had, remaine shut vp within the bare walls of a poore chamber, hauing not wherewithall to allay the rage of hunger, nor scarcely to couer nakednesse. There are others, who, for the space of three dayes together haue not gotten a morsell of bread to put into their mouthes. Wee haue iust cause to feare, that some doe perish for want of food: others for want of tendance: others for want of ordinary helpes and remedies, with which they might easily escape death, and be cured. At this present there are aboue fifty seuerall families, which are visited, and shut vp; and truly such is the feeling, which many of these poore creatures haue, of this their most wretched estate, that finding themselues depriued of meanes whereby to liue, (all manner of worke fayling them at this time) they are brought euen to the brinke of despaire, wishing from their heart to be ceaz'd vpon with the sicknesse (if God were so pleased) thereby to hasten death, and with it, the end of this their languishing paine, which to them is worse then death it selfe.

The example of the Protestants, both in the City and the Countrey (which is well knowne to all) may bee no small inducement vnto Catholicks, to imitate their care, prouidence, and bounty in this behalfe. We haue heard of some particulers amongst them, which are very memorable. One noble man of theirs hath bestowed lately the summe of three hundred pounds, leauing it to the distribution of a Gentleman of good quality, who tooke the paines to visit the houses of the poore himselfe, and to deuide it amongst them with his owne hands. An other party of account (Sonne to an Alderman of London) hath beene seene to goe in person to seeke out the poore that wanted worke, being neighbours to such as were infected, and with his owne hands to bestow a large beneuolence amongst them. And if those who acknowledge no merit in good workes, out of a generous minde, or naturall compassion are so ready to assist their distressed brethren so plentifully; it may seeme that no lesse, but rather much more should bee expected at the hands of Catholicks, who professing, to belieue the doctrine of merit, haue thereby a farre higher motiue than Protestants haue to performe workes of Charity, and to open the bowells of mercy, especially in a time of so generall and pressing necessity, towards their poore and desolate brethren, who haue no expectation or hope of reliefe from any, but from them alone.

This publicke Declaration wee haue iudged necessary to make to all English Catholicks, particulerly to those that are of ability, for the discharge of our owne soules, requesting, or rather coniuring all in generall, and euery one in particular by the bowells of our Sauiour Iesus Christ to make it their owne case, and to haue that saying of S. *Iohn* the Euangelist alwayes before their eyes, *He that shall haue the substance of the world, and shall see his brother haue neede, and shall shut his bowels from him; how doth the Charity of God abide in him?*

6. of October, 1636.

Permissu Superiorum.

L. S. H. M.

HENRY MORSE'S APPEAL "TO THE CATHOLICKES OF ENGLAND"

An Apothecary's Shop

A Doctor's Dispensary

'refresh their spirit, exhausted after unremitting occupation and anxieties'. 'So in solitary and uninterrupted meditation for several days', says Fr. Alegambe, 'Morse prepared himself for the field of struggle', and at the end of his retreat 'renewed his vows and with fresh fervour offered himself wholly to God, to take his life more than sixty times, if that were possible.'

After allowing for his extravagant manner of expression, it can be seen that Fr. Alegambe wished clearly to emphasise that his friend and former pupil offered himself unreservedly to the work, gladly and regardless of the cost in health or life.

Back in London, Morse found the plague spreading without check. The city was stricken with fear. Tragically, almost comically, the poor people in their ignorance and alarm hesitated to eat or go out or speak with their neighbour lest they should catch the plague. Self-styled observers who 'had conversed with the infected' to find out 'the nature, origin, and ways of curing the plague' noted how each individual caught the infection. A curious list, published in a widely-read pamphlet, counted more than seventy causes. An entire family, the author noted, had perished from drinking small beer in an over-heated room; an old lady, recently dead, had eaten red cherries, another a cucumber, a third a dish of eels, and so on, through codling tart, cream and gooseberry fool to the fat near the rump of a loin of mutton. The tales were believed, although the list left scarcely a single food for those who sought immunity. Contradictions in experience did not matter. To sit up too late dried and inflamed the blood and so weakened nature's resistance; water was as dangerous as dead beer; to go hungry as to over-eat; the infection could be caught as easily through an east window as by keeping a chamber close.

The people were in panic; and the pretence of scientific inquiry into the manner of infection did nothing to allay it. The official recommendations of the Royal College of Physicians, issued in the spring, showed almost equal ignorance of science. Convinced that infection was carried on the air, they recommended street bonfires. As in the plague of 1625, every householder in London had to lay sufficient pitch and faggots in the street for three fires a week. The remedy dated from the time of Hippocrates, who was said to have relieved a plague-ridden city by setting fire to a wood that encircled it. Day and night the medicinal smoke and stench added foulness to the city. It was part of the watchmen's task to keep the street fires burning and to hold their flames within safe distance of the overhanging timber houses. While the fires flared in the streets, the cannon of the Tower were daily fired in an effort to 'correct the infectious air'.

Within the shut-in houses a suffocating odour of stale perfumes was created at considerable expense, for these were used liberally both for the room and the person. Sorrel and sage, with leaves of rue, were recommended as flavouring for a simple diet of bread. It was believed also that London treacle, a remedy first used in the Black Death, fortified the skin against sores.

In the streets the embers of the dead fires mingled with the unswept scourings of the sick rooms. The provision of rakers in normal times was inadequate: but now they disappeared altogether from the London scene. Massed dirt was left un-touched at the doorways of abandoned dwellings: in 'visited' houses the occupants were forbidden to emerge, even to sweep the pavement. As the plague advanced with the summer the condition of the city grew worse.

It was a happy hunting-ground for vermin. There was no difficulty in enforcing the order to destroy 'cats, dogs, conies and tame pigeons', and to restrict swine 'from ranging up and down the streets', but the principal carriers were undoubtedly the rats. They fattened in the unkempt streets and in the un-

ventilated locked-up tenements. No attention was paid to
them. It was not the common brown rat that lives and breeds
now in wharfs and warehouses, but its predecessor, the English
or black rat, almost extinct in towns, a smaller creature, living
close to man in huts and houses. It bred and fattened in the
plague-ridden city, with its uncollected garbage, for all other
scavengers had been destroyed by orders. It was regarded with
least suspicion, and with great ease it made its runs through the
lath and plaster walls of the timbered houses.[1]

In the absence from London of most persons who normally
held authority—justices of the peace, aldermen and constables—lawlessness increased. Many thousands of suspicious
people roamed the suburbs 'apt to enter any desperate action'.
Masters of the London trades who had fled for safety to the
country left behind their apprentices and servants 'who became
rudely wanton'. The popular belief that venereal disease gave
immunity from the plague led to lewd scenes in the streets.
There was little other occupation left in the almost total
paralysis of trade. Many thousands of watermen, porters,
hackney coachmen and discarded Irish footmen in 'very desperate condition' drifted into suburbs like St. Giles-in-the-
Fields where alone they could get lodgings. Tailors, shoe-
makers, glovers and silk-weavers, unable to feed their servants,
dismissed them to roam the streets. By October the lawlessness in the streets was so increased that it was suggested that a
Provost Master General should be appointed with powers 'to
scour the suburbs' of all who had swollen the mass of city
rogues and vagabonds.

It was a crime to attempt to escape from the city. If any

[1] The home of the 'English' rat was the East, where the plague had its
origin. In the eighteenth century it was largely driven out by the stronger
Norwegian or Hanoverian brown rat, which lived more remotely in
sewers. With the virtual extinction of the English or black rat, the plague
ceased.

person with an unhealed plague sore on his body was found abroad, either in the streets or on the roads leading out of the city, he could be made 'to suffer the pains of death as in case of felony'; if he had no sores, he could be 'whipped as a vagabond and bound to good behaviour'. Nevertheless, many poor persons, maddened by their imprisonment, broke out from London, often to die on the road or to be driven back to the city by watchers, who stood armed with bills and halberds at the entrance to the villages through which they passed. In a tract written during the outbreak of 1625, and reissued with revisions in 1636, John Taylor describes the fate of the refugees sleeping wherever possible in stables, barns or outhouses to avoid the village watchmen.

> The name of London now both far and near
> Strikes all the towns and villages with fear.

And he chastised the country dwellers, concerned only for their own safety:

> Uncharitable hounds, hearts hard as rock,
> Who suffer people in the field to sink
> Rather than give or sell a draught of drink.

He did not exaggerate. There was the case of a man, in convulsions from the plague, lying desperate on the river bank at Maidenhead. Two of the townspeople hurled stones at him; then 'with a boat-hook they hitched the wretch in his breeches, dragged him backwards with his face grovelling on the ground, to a place under the bridge, where they left him until the fit passed and he could continue his journey'. Nearer London, at Richmond, a plague-stricken man was drawn out naked from his house by his wife and boy and thrown into the river, where his corpse was found the next day.

London was at warfare with the surrounding countryside. The scene described by John Donne in 1625 was repeated this year. 'The citizens fled as from a house on fire and stuffed their pockets with their best ware, and were not received so much as in barns, and perished so; some of them with more money about them than would have bought the village where they died. A justice of the peace told me of one that died with £1,400 about him.' The tradesmen led the flight. Business was dead; they had nothing to lose by leaving the city. In June 1636 the Council, settled now with the King at Hampton Court, complained to Archbishop Laud at Croydon that 'multitudes of tradesmen and others flying into the country towns' were already settled there. An order was given that no lodgers should be permitted at Hampton Court; special houses were to be found for Londoners, and if this proved impossible, they should 'be sent back to the city or removed to other places'. In Greenwich, where the King kept his house, and at Oatlands, where he intended to reside in the summer, similar orders were given; Havering Park and Wanstead, resorts where he planned short sojourns, were cleared of Londoners. When a case of plague was reported at Teddington, all persons in the infected house were removed to a greater distance from the Court. But in spite of repeated prohibitions, John Warner, a wharfinger of Chertsey, Surrey, continued to ply his barges between Hampton Court and London. Only a summons to appear before the Council put an end to his traffic. Even at Kingston 'the houses infected were not kept shut up', the Council complained, 'nor was the red cross or any other mark set on them, nor any watch set on them to keep the people therein from going forth or others from visiting them'. Only in October, when the plague reached its peak, sterner measures were taken, and London became a sealed city.

10

THE DYING AND THE DEAD

THE sealing-up of infected houses was a tragic measure. In St. Giles-in-the-Fields the crowded tenements were occupied by four or sometimes five families, frequently strangers to one another. No exit was permitted once a case of the plague had been reported. Barred in behind doors fastened with padlock and staple, the healthy and the infected lived side by side. The wisdom of the order had never been questioned. First enforced by Cardinal Wolsey in 1518, it had now the sanction of the College of Physicians, who considered contagion inescapable. Although there were cases to prove the contrary, it was argued that anyone who came into contact with a plague victim was certain to fall sick himself. Thus, without work or occupation, the healthy were forced to await the death of each victim in turn. No food or medicine was available except such as the parish visitors brought them; or, in the case of Catholics, the two priests assigned to this work. 'I sent for Mr. Morse when I was visited with the plague,' testified Margaret Allen, a poor woman of St. Giles-in-the-Fields, 'and he many times gave alms to me, my husband and my two little children, who all died of the plague, the parish not giving us anything, we being very poor and seven persons in number shut up.' In desperation often both the sick and the healthy in a plague-stricken house forcibly made their escape. More often they failed to report their sickness; thus the plague spread abroad and the death-roll increased. The only lawful refuge, appalling always and inadequate after the first weeks of the visitation, was the pest-house. But for the whole of the city and its outlying parishes there was one permanent pest-house. A second was later built at Westminster, and a third, a timber structure on a foundation course of brick, in St. Giles-in-the-Fields. There a well was sunk for water, and the hut walled in and guarded by watchers. As the keeper accepted payment from each parish that sent in their sick, few Catholics entered; and in any case, the pest-houses of Westminster and St. Giles had space for no more than sixty persons. Shutting up was the alternative.

Like the officials who visited the infected houses, Morse bore a 'distinctive mark on his outer garment' and carried a white rod in his hand 'that others might avoid his company'. Each week when a list of the sick was presented to the parish, he transcribed their names into a notebook. It was insisted that the victims should be buried immediately after death, but always between nightfall and sunrise and in places apart. After the burial the visitors would return to the house where the death had occurred and burn all the clothes and bedding used by the dead person. Compensation to registered parishioners was provided by the parish funds: but Morse had to make replacements from his own resources. Also, he had to find the medicines, hear the confessions of the sick, and, if they were dying, bring them viaticum. After their death he would lay out the corpse to be buried. 'Day and night he worked,' writes Fr. Alegambe, 'and although he gave his principal attention to Catholics, he did not neglect others. It is hardly credible what hard work and horrors he endured. All the time he was in close contact with the plague-stricken, entering rooms that were oppressive with foul and pestilential air, sitting down beside a bed in the midst of squalor of the most repulsive and contagious nature,' to exhort sinners to make a confession before they died.

Morse was particularly sensitive to the odours of the shut-up victims of the plague. In the first days of his attendance on the sick he incurred the outspoken censure of his fellow-priest, John Southworth. 'Whether overpowered at the outset by the noisome symptoms of the disease', one biographer writes, 'or anxious to leave none of the daily increasing number of patients without the most essential help, he was satisfied with administering the sacraments of Penance and the Holy Eucharist, and omitted Extreme Unction.' Fr. Southworth heard of this. At once he complained to the Chapter of the 'unworthy timidity' of his fellow-worker. Indeed Morse may have found it too repellent to bend over the dying victims and sign with his anointing thumb their putrid sores on the forehead, lips, nose and ears. Anyhow he accepted the rebuke. He blamed himself for lack of courage, and henceforth gave all the sacraments to the dying.

The accusation of Fr. Southworth may indeed have been true. In the belief that the plague was carried on the air, windows were tightly fastened to keep out the infection, or within the building even keyholes were blocked up to keep it confined to the sick-room. For days before his visits no fresh air would have been admitted to the sick quarters. At the height of a very hot summer faggot-fires—more fragrant than coal—were kept burning night and day by the bed of the sick, and pungent disinfectants—nitre, tar and rosin—placed on the flames. In the poorer houses old shoes and scraps of leather and horn were used as a substitute.

It is more probable that Morse was anxious to make a first preliminary census of all Catholics who had fallen victims of the plague. For it attacked people in different ways. Most commonly the first symptom was a sudden loss of strength;

and this was followed by death sometimes within twenty-four hours, often on the second or third day. With others it took a slower course. But Fr. Morse, familiar with plague cases from his experience in Newcastle, may have been anxious first to confess all the victims before returning a second time to administer the sacrament of Extreme Unction. If this is the correct understanding of the dispute, he acted rightly.

The first funds for the relief of Catholics were soon exhausted. Food, medicines, nurses, replacements of burnt clothing, the maintenance of whole families deprived of their livelihood—all had to be found. At first collections were made merely in London. The Queen contributed; but still more money was required. In October Morse and Southworth jointly issued an appeal to Catholics of the whole kingdom. It was dated the sixth of the month, three days after the Middlesex justices at a General Sessions of the Peace had confessed that the plague-stricken parishes could no longer support the whole burden of their relief and had taxed a further sixty-three parishes in the county. Morse, of course, could appeal only to charity. 'Having seen with our eyes', wrote the two priests, 'the extreme necessity which many of the poorer sort are fallen into' we 'do think ourselves obliged even in conscience' to make their need known to all. They continued: 'We do protest to you seriously, even upon our souls and consciences, that the greatness of the calamity exceedeth all belief, insomuch as we should never have imagined in the least part of that which really is, had not our own eyes and daily experience attested the same unto us.' They pointed out that 'the small means and power we have to relieve them'—namely, the gifts made by Catholics who remained in the stricken city —were insufficient to meet 'so great a desolation among our poor brethren'. For lack of funds they could not give the help that was needed; and this is 'a far more grievous affliction to us than all the labours and dangers we undergo daily for their spiritual aid and comfort'.

The phrasing and manner of the appeal resemble the pages of Morse's journal. In the third paragraph he recounts his experiences, giving perhaps the most authentic picture of London in time of plague. 'There are some persons in the number of these afflicted, who notwithstanding they are wellborn and bred, having been constrained through extremity of want to sell or pawn all they had, remain shut up within the bare walls of a poor chamber, having not wherewithal to allay the rage of hunger, nor scarcely to cover nakedness. There are others, who for the space of three days together have not gotten a morsel of bread to put into their mouths. We have just cause to fear that some do perish for want of food; others for want of tendance; others for want of ordinary helps and remedies, with which they might easy escape death and be cured. . . . And truly such is the feeling which many of these poor creatures have of this their most wretched state, that finding themselves deprived of means whereby to live—all manner of work failing them at this time—they are brought even to the brink of despair, wishing from their heart to be seized upon with the sickness (if God were so pleased), thereby to hasten death, and, with it, the end of this their languishing pain, which to them is worse than death itself.'

Morse appealed to duty, not to charity. He praised the generosity and self-sacrifice of Protestants, men who did not believe in the doctrine of merit. Since they showed such readiness to assist their brethren, Catholics, whose faith gave them more forcible motives, should not be left behind. The passage has great interest: 'The example of Protestants, both in the city and in the country (which is well known to all) may be no small inducement unto Catholics to imitate their care, providence and bounty in this behalf. We have heard of some particulars amongst them, which are very memorable. One nobleman of theirs hath bestowed lately the sum of three hundred pounds, leaving it to the distribution of a gentleman of good quality, who took the pains to visit the houses of the poor himself and to divide it amongst them with his own hands. Another party of account (son to an alderman of London) hath been seen to go in person to seek out the poor that wanted work . . . and with his own hands to bestow a large benevolence amongst them. And if those who acknowledge no merit in good works, out of a generous mind or natural compassion are so ready to assist their distressed brethren so plentifully, it may seem that no less, but rather much more, should be expected at the hands of Catholics, who professing to believe the doctrine of merit, have thereby a far higher motive than Protestants have to perform works of charity and to open the bowels of mercy, especially in a time of so general and pressing necessity, towards their poor desolate brethren, who have no expectation or hope of relief from any but them alone.'

It is the argument perhaps of a convert, who as a student had heard the controversial question of merit and good works discussed at the Inns of Court and had sought to resolve it at Douai in the days before his reception into the Church.

The appeal ends fittingly with a quotation from St. John: 'He that shall have the substance of the world and shall see his brother have need, and shall shut his bowels from him, how doth the charity of God abide in him?'

The response again was generous. Throughout the country collections were made among Catholic congregations. Hitherto a few wealthy Catholic families who had remained in London had borne the burden. Many of them, in order to give more generously to the relief of their co-religionists, had refused to contribute to the parish collections. In May, five

months before the appeal, the justices of the peace in Middlesex
had made out a long list of Catholics dwelling in Clerkenwell
who 'had refused to contribute to the relief of the infected'.
Among them were Lady Gage, Sir John Symonds, Lady May,
Mr. Ballard and his wife, the Lady Resby—all of whom had
answered Morse's first local appeal for funds.

The principal contributor to the new fund was again the
Queen. It is not known whether Morse was personally
acquainted with her, but she took a close interest in his work,
and later extended her protection to him. Her first gift was five
hundred gold crowns. Other gifts followed from her treasury,
and thus the fund became known among the poor as her
Majesty's alms. 'I being a poor labouring woman', testified
Elizabeth Godwin of St. Giles-in-the-Fields, 'never did or was
able to keep a servant, and being shut up seven weeks, buried
three of my little children, which Mr. Morse relieved with her
Majesty's and with divers Catholics' alms.' This was a typical
testimony given at Morse's trial. There can be no doubt that
without this fund the mortality among the Catholic poor would
have been still greater; the same woman concluded: 'otherwise
we had perished' since 'six persons of us were shut up for
seven weeks and never had of the parish but five shillings'.
Another Catholic, Edward Freshwater, a labourer in the parish,
told a similar story. Through a window—the watchers had
refused him entrance—Morse handed him some money. For
eight weeks he was shut up with his family. Only twice during
this time was his door unfastened from the outside, when the
buriers' cart came to gather the dead bodies of his two little
children. Before summoning Morse, he was forced by his 'extreme poverty', as he said, to beg from Mr. Wilson, a constable
of St. Giles-in-the-Fields. At first Wilson refused help, but
was finally persuaded to give the family twenty-two shillings
'by way of loan, compelling me to pay him the same again'.

Possibly Wilson, the constable, was misled by Puritan preachers who, groping for a cause of the plague, ascribed it to the idolatry, practised by the Papists. The simple-minded people among the poorer classes of London gave unhesitating credence to Puritan ranters. Chief among them was Dr. Gouge, who declared that the principal cause of the plague was God's anger at the growth of Catholicism. When he surveyed the progress that Catholics had made in the last twenty years, he saw a desperate need 'to inculcate the apostolic prohibition, *Flee from Idolatry*'. In the previous reign the bright light of the gospel had dispelled the thick cloud of Popery; now, 'in many places that cloud gathereth and thickeneth again'. He prayed God it might not increase 'as the cloud which Eliah's servant espied, which at first, though it were but a little one, like a man's hand, yet it grew to cover the whole sky'. Already Morse had made many converts. In the violence of religious feeling, his success and that of other London priests was linked with the manifestation of God's present anger. 'Too many seducers are among us; too great countenance is given to them', cried Gouge, with a fanaticism that was exploited at Morse's trial and assisted his conviction.

Other preachers made the established Church a scapegoat for the plague equally with the Papists. In a christening sermon, preached on Jeremiah viii, 20—*the harvest is past, the summer is ended and we are not saved*—Mr. Sparrock, lecturer at Woolchurch, inveighed against 'the cursed adorations and bowing at names' introduced into Church ceremonies. Without hesitation he stated that 'the plague of God was in the land for the new mixtures of religion that is commanded in Churches'. Londoners were always susceptible to mass emotion; and, as many instances show, both Morse and Southworth were often harassed in their work by officials and citizens who saw in them the agents of antichrist.

More malicious than the obstruction caused by Puritans, was the mischief made by other Catholics. In the worst months of the plague, Peter Fitton, back now from Rome and a member of the London Chapter, appears to have instigated a fresh dispute between Morse and Southworth.

The question at issue was Morse's 'faculties' for hearing confessions.

By an arrangement dating from the time of Edmund Campion's mission in 1580 the Jesuits crossing to England received their 'faculties' direct from the Holy See. This privilege had been unquestioned until 1624. In that year Richard Smith, Bishop of Chalcedon, had set up an episcopal chapter and, at the same time, claimed sole right to grant 'faculties' to priests in England. It was the first move to get the Jesuits out of England and was linked with Fitton's rebellion in Rome. The Bishop's visit lasted little over a year. Although the Holy See had accepted his resignation and quashed his disputed measures the chapter continued its existence and claimed the rights asserted by the Bishop. Fitton now advanced Smith's work. He persuaded Fr. Southworth, a simple priest, to spread word that Fr. Morse had no true 'faculties' and that consequently all the confessions he had heard were invalid.

In anger Morse sought out his fellow-worker. He was prepared to have his moral courage called in question, but it was another matter to allow the poor Catholics of St. Giles to have their peace of soul destroyed on their bed of agony. In strong protest he pointed out that the chapter knew that the Holy See had granted the Jesuits their 'faculties': at any time it was disloyal to call the grant in question, and more than mischievous to do so at such a time as this.

There was no further quarrel between the two priests. Southworth now worked with heroism, principally in the heavily infected city of Westminster, which was built mainly on marshland, and had no drainage except the open ditches which received every kind of pollution. Within the shadow of the great Abbey were foul-smelling courts and passages, dilapidated slums, and poor streets like Petty France ending abruptly at the marshes through which the river Tyburn flowed into the Thames. On the north side of the Abbey, lay the worst tenements of London—Bell Alley, a stifling cul-de-sac with decaying timber buildings separated by a thin thread of flagstones; on the north-west was Thieving Alley, another notorious plague-spot. Here the plague was intermittent throughout the reign, and the mortality figures as great as in St. Giles-in-the-Fields. In 1625 alone more than fifteen hundred plague deaths had been recorded in Westminster, though the actual number was certainly greater.

About four weeks before Morse and Southworth published their joint appeal, Morse fell sick for the first time. It was the feast of Our Lady's nativity 1636. He had been busy that day hearing confessions of the sick and administering the last sacraments. On his return to his lodgings, he felt the first symptoms of the plague—the sense of weariness with the slight shivering and giddiness. A Catholic doctor, Thomas Turner, who knew Morse well and had worked with him since the beginning of the outbreak, was immediately called. He prescribed a nightly sweat. Although Morse continued to work during the day—the need and numbers of the sick allowed him no respite—very slowly he recovered sufficient strength to resume his customary night calls.

For the most part the official watchers at the doors of infected houses allowed the two priests to visit the Catholic sick unimpeded. Morse, however, was more fortunate than Southworth, who was closely watched by Mr. Robert White, the sub-curate of St. Margaret's. 'Under pretence of distributing alms', White protested to the Council, 'Southworth took occasion to go into visited houses' and there seduced the parishioners from their allegiance to the King's religion. As instances he mentioned William Baldwin and William Styles, both dwelling in Hemp Yard, Westminster. 'Finding Baldwin at the point of death', White continued, Southworth 'set upon him to make him change his religion, whereunto he consented and received the sacraments from the Church of Rome.' It was a genuine case of conversion, but there were many others whom the priests attended merely to bestow 'the Queen's bounty' as a supplement to their parish allowance. Nevertheless, a single case was enough to disturb the sub-curate. 'To hide his practices', he explained, Southworth 'fees the watchmen to affirm that he comes only to give alms.' In fact, he was 'unsettling poor people in their religion', and, what was more serious, was bringing the Queen's life into danger. 'Many of these newly turned Catholics' attended Mass at Denmark House. It was a matter for the Council to prohibit, for they would spread infection at Court.

The charges later made against Morse went further. It is certain that he made many converts among the sick and dying. The exact number cannot be determined. Of fifteen cases of poor people who were alleged to have changed their religion at his instigation, all proved to have been lifelong Catholics. Cecily Crowe's reply under examination is typical. She was a widow, 'aged four-score years or thereabouts, dwelling in Bloomsbury'. It had been said that she, her son and two daughters, were 'drawn to the Roman religion' by Fr. Morse. 'I take my oath', she protested, 'that many years before I knew him I was a Roman Catholic, and that my two daughters accused to have been perverted by him, are both Protestants. True it is that I sent to him to come to me when I was visited with the sickness and shut up; and being ready to starve I received comfort and relief many times from our gracious

Queen by his means, the parish not giving us anything because we were recusants, notwithstanding Catholics did contribute liberally to the officers of the parish towards relief in this time of sickness.' Her son, Anthony, likewise testified on oath that as he had been 'always a Roman Catholic, the information that Mr. Morse perverted me is false'.

Morse visited Protestant and Catholic alike. Many parish officials had left the city; the burden on those that remained was greater than they could efficiently carry. Besides, there were others who neglected their duties and preachers who defended their cowardice, particularly Richard Kephale. With the pretence of thorough research into the Scriptures, he had claimed during an earlier outbreak that he could find there 'no ground to bind public persons to hazard themselves in particular men's cases'; and now in the worst months of the plague his mischievous pamphlet, *Medela Pestilentiae*, was republished, dedicated to the Lord Mayor and sheriffs of London. Arguing that officials, both civic and parochial, 'are set over society, not over one or two particular persons', he concluded that the 'whole civic body would suffer if their life were taken away by infection'. While Morse, in his appeal for funds, stated the traditional doctrine that true faith was proved by works of charity, several Protestant ministers, following Kephale, sought in Scripture excuses for their neglect of the sick. In consequence the poor suffered grievously. In April 1636 the Council had been forced to threaten their arrest: 'If there be any person, ecclesiastical or lay, that shall hold or publish any opinions that it is a vain thing to forbear to resort to the infected . . . pretending that no person shall die but at the time prefixed, he shall be apprehended.'

In the lack of adequate organisation for relief the poorest people were neglected. To them as well as to the Catholics Fr. Morse ministered. His kindness made many converts—it was claimed that he received five hundred into the Church during the plague. Although later the Council paid tribute to his Christian behaviour, nevertheless it was treason in law to 'seduce anyone from the religion established by law'.

There was the case, for example, of the young Protestant girl who had summoned Morse at night. Sick with the plague, she wished to be received immediately into the Church. But she was already dead when the priest reached her house. Her mother, seeing Morse's distress, inquired the cause; and before the priest had left the house had herself asked to be instructed. But little could be kept secret among the poor. 'Her heretic neighbours,' the account continues, 'getting knowledge of this, gathered before her door and begged her, by the bonds of her ancient friendships, not to abandon her old beliefs. Courageously the woman answered them, that even if she should be torn to pieces by wild horses, she would never forsake the Catholic faith, in which alone there was hope of salvation.' As with other converts, the assistance received from the public alms was withdrawn. Eventually, however, an exception was made in her favour, for she was exceedingly poor. Later Morse received her surviving children into the Church. This done, she caught the plague and died.

Eventually, at the end of October Mr. White, sub-curate of St. Margaret's, secured the arrest of Fr. Southworth. Sir Dudley Carlton, the Clerk of the Council, directed a warrant to the keeper of the Gatehouse prison, Westminster, to take him into custody and detain him in prison, although, as the priest protested, he had 'laboured only to preserve the poor from perishing, which he thought would offend neither his Majesty nor the State'. For the rest of the winter, during which the plague reached its peak, Fr. Morse was left alone.

I I

INCREASE AND DECLINE

FIVE months before Fr. Southworth's arrest the prisoners in the debtors' prison of the Fleet had been given liberty to seek the country. 'The destroying angel has begun to stretch his hand over the city and this close prison is in the greatest danger', the debtors petitioned the King on 29 May. Moreover, they urged that their death 'would deprive their creditors of all hope of satisfaction and his Majesty of dutiful and hereafter useful subjects'. Accordingly the next day orders were given for their release under *habeas corpus*. The same mercy was shown the Southwark debtors in the King's Bench prison. In Newgate, the Gatehouse and the Clink and other gaols north of the river no such reprieve was granted. There the inmates stayed throughout the plague. In May the first notifications of plague-deaths were returned from the Clink; others had died in the Gatehouse before Southworth was taken into custody there in October. Indeed, in the overcrowded, ill-ventilated quarters of the London gaols the inmates stood little chance of escaping the contagion. John Southworth was more fortunate than the rest: he kept free of the sickness, and after a time seems even to have continued his work discreetly in the Westminster slums, returning at evening to the Gatehouse, near the west entrance to the Abbey.[1]

[1] Fr. John Southworth was eventually executed at Tyburn on 28 June 1654. His quartered and mummified body is now preserved and venerated at Westminster Cathedral.

In October the plague reached its peak. More deaths were recorded in the week ending the twentieth than in any previous or later period. Looking back on the rise and decline of mortality in 1636, in the hope of forecasting a similar course for the great plague in 1666, Dr. Gadbury observed: 'In the year 1636, towards the end of April, when the sun came to the opposite point of Mars in the figure of the world, the plague then first began.' In this he was incorrect, for the plague had then already become so widespread that Morse and Southworth had been chosen that month to look after the Catholic sick of London. Nevertheless, he continued: 'In May and June, when the sun came to the opposite point of the ascendant, Venus to the opposite point of Saturn, and afterwards to the Dragon's tail, it increased but not much.' Actually the number of deaths in June had been more than double the deaths in May. Undeterred Gadbury pursued his argument. 'In September and October, the months in which the plague most of all increased, Mars was in the ascendant upon the quadrate place of the moon, and afterwards passed to the quadrate place of the sun and the conjunctional place of Saturn . . . all of which were causes of the increase the plague then had.' Indeed all was explained by the heavenly location of 'the furious and hostile beams of the fiery planet Mars, for in November 1636 Jupiter came to the sextile of its ascendant and the sun in time to his own place; then the pestilence began to grow less raging and by degrees decreased to almost nothing'.

A less credulous observer, Morse noticed that the cold winter that followed the raging summer had more to do with the very gradual decline of the plague than any movements of celestial bodies. If in August it 'greatly increased' and in September and October 'most of all', there were simpler causes than those proposed by Gadbury.

But Morse worked from day to day without speculating on

planetary influences. Although in November there were fewer plague-deaths than in October, his work did not become easier. From now on he was harassed by sickness and trouble-makers. He was alone. His recovery had been far from complete. He had allowed himself no convalescence nor even any remission from his work during the day or night.

It was at this crisis of the plague that something near miraculous occurred. All the biographers are agreed on this. The incident, perhaps, is best told in their words:

'He never spared himself, and a short time after recovering from his first sickness, he felt the plague on him again, this time much more severely. Immediately the Superior of the London district wrote to him. He ordered Fr. Morse to give up altogether his work for the plague-stricken. He was to rest until he had made a complete recovery. The Superior told him at the same time that he had asked all his brethren in England to pray for his recovery. And now, the very moment he had finished reading the letter—Fr. Morse himself called this a marvellous occurrence—he passed the crisis of his sickness and was conscious that the danger of death had gone. Although naturally he made use of all the assistance the doctor could provide to rid himself of the effects of the plague, still it was at this exact moment that he began to get completely well.'

Morse's physician, Dr. Thomas Turner, was a Catholic. He and another Catholic, Dr. More, had attended the sick throughout the plague. These two men, with other Catholic physicians in London, worked in co-operation with Morse. Theirs was the only profession from which Catholics were not rigidly excluded. Qualification at home, in London or the two Universities, was made difficult at times; nevertheless no obstacles were put in the way of their practising. Turner had qualified at Padua, the best medical school in Europe, where Dr. More had been appointed a lecturer on taking his degree.

Both were members of the Royal College of Physicians,
devout Catholics, with brothers among the English priests.
In spite of the danger of contagion, Turner himself attended
Morse. But the priest objected; he was taking an unwarranted
risk. Turner insisted. Morse then urged a fellow-priest who
was with him to send the doctor away; but it was no use. 'I
must do it', Turner protested. 'Of course I am taking a risk,
but after all it is just what the Father has been doing every day
and night for months.' With his own hands he softened the
carbuncles on the priest's body; then he lanced them. It was
his duty, he said, to serve personally a priest who had devoted
himself to saving the lives of the poor. 'If I acted otherwise I
would be unworthy of all the Catholic medical men in London.'

After the operation Morse offered the doctor the customary
fee. Turner returned it as an alms for the sick. For several days
he continued to visit Morse till he was recovered.

The large number of Catholic doctors in attendance on the
London sick helped to reduce the wasteful expenditure by the
poor on quack medicines. Morse carried with him from house
to house the usual remedies recommended by the College of
Physicians. He was shocked at the large sums the poor spent
on worthless pills and lozenges. Still, in ignorance and in fran-
tic search for immunity or cure, the sick of London assured the
quacks of brisk business. The most unscrupulous trader was
Stephen Bradwell. He had been busy in the plague of 1625.
His influence was greater than other merchants for he had a
smattering of medical knowledge and a much-vaunted family
business, as well as a persuasive pen to promote the sales of his
wares. *A Watchman for the Pest, Teaching the True Rules of
Preservation from the Contagion* was a classic among the ignor-
ant; but in his introduction he did speak truly: 'Poor people,
by reason of their great want, living sluttishly, feeding nastily
on offals, on the waste and unwholesome meats, and many

times, too, lacking food altogether, have both their bodies much corrupted and their spirit exceedingly weakened,' and for this reason 'they become of all others much subject to this sickness'. Bradwell, in fact, had seen 'the plague sweep up such people in great heaps'. To them he now offered his 'excellent electuary', his lozenges and rich pomanders. As he was known to have failed his degree in medicine at Oxford, he wisely advertised all these remedies as made according to the prescription of his grandfather, an Elizabethan practitioner: and he claimed, with concern only for his sales, that they had 'been proved effectual both by his and my father's experience'. Sitting in his 'study in Mugwell Street', he surveyed the distress of London. 'I confess these remedies are costly, but slight means and cheap medicines, however they promise, prove as dear as death.' So great was his reputation that other tradesmen, such as 'a fellow in Distaff Lane', boosted their pills by asserting that they had been made on the recipe of Bradwell's grandfather. In days before the system of patents gave legal protection, Bradwell could only resort to obloquy: any fellow 'bragging of a medicine that was my grandfather's' was a downright liar, for 'my grandfather was very scrupulous of giving any special receipts to others. But if any man can say that he has any receipt of his, I am sure, if it is of any value, I have a copy of it.' Indeed, he had a 'whole volume of excellent receipts' left him by his forebears, and, afraid the poor might regard him as 'too strict and covetous', he divulged 'for the common good' one prescription, of which the ingredients were unobtainable in London. This gesture of generosity, therefore, in no way impaired the sales of his electuary or antiloymon, which he sold at two shillings an ounce and his 'liquor of Life', priced at five shillings a pint. Besides these remedies for the rich, he had to offer perfumes for airing clothes, sweet waters for sponges, and others to cast on a hot fire-shovel, 'all temperate and catholick, that is, generally fit for all constitutions'. To the poor he could only sell his 'powder of life' at threepence a grain; its virtues, he confessed, were beyond his 'modesty of expression'. So, between his shop in Golden Lane and his study in Mugwell Street, he maligned other traders—like Samuel Speed at the Rainbow near the Inner Temple gate, who marketed a seed packet which had an immense variety of uses as a preservative against anything from the pestilence to Essex sea-fogs.

Tragically, as the poet Taylor wrote, these quacks 'picked up their living from other men's dying'. He complained that the London buildings were plastered with their heartless advertisements:

> On many a post I see the quack-salvers' bills
> Like fencers' challenges to show their skill.

Although certain mountebanks among the physicians had got hold of good herbal prescriptions, the loud boosting of their more worthless remedies checked the sale of the cheaper and more genuine medicines. All that the physicians could do to check the quacks was to recommend thick London treacle morning and evening. But even here they met with competition, for the quacks claimed special mixtures, which cured both venereal disease and plague sores.

It is not known how many days Morse remained sick in his lodgings. After Dr. Turner had lanced his sores he began to recover. As he was still 'weak and unwell' when he resumed his work, he was probably not more than four or five days away from the sick.

It was now late October. With the approach of winter the daily total of deaths very slowly decreased, but it was only in the new year that the authorities could be certain that the worst was past. When, at the end of February, Henry Morse was again arrested, he wrote: 'Now, for nearly the whole winter, I have attended alone to the wants of the plague-stricken Catholics—from the time of my own happy recovery.' Southworth was in the Gatehouse and had not been replaced. Morse could not delay his return to work so long as he could drag himself through the city of the dying. His strength was just sufficient. It was only in the damp chambers at Newgate, when his work was over, that he felt the plague on him again.

In the winter months the laws were enforced more effectively. During the previous summer no regulations could stop clandestine assemblies for sport. There had been no difficulty in cancelling plays or the churchyard sermons at Bethlehem gate on Whit-Sunday, or at St. Peter's fair on St. Peter's day at Westminster, but bear-baiting and buckler play had continued in the back-alleys. Now, with the coming of winter, they ceased; also ballad-singing and the hawking of wares in the streets. There were no assemblies now of any kind; the courts were in abeyance, no jurymen were summoned, no inquests held. Writing- and grammar-schools were closed, also institutions for fencing-lessons and dancing. Only travelling guests were received at inns; residents of the district were compelled to collect their food or drink and carry it back to consume in their houses; passing strangers only were served at the door. At the Thames-side wharfs beggars were refused landing, and a special watch was set to prevent the sale of what the city authorities condemned as 'stinking fish, unwholesome meat and must corn'. Finally, and only after taking the extreme measure of closing all paper-mills in London and the county of Middlesex, the Council put an end to the dangerous traffic in rags, old clothes and refuse sold to paper manufacturers. Rag-gatherers were now punished as rogues, and justices were empowered to visit the cellars of poor houses and bury or burn rags piled up for the visit of the rag-gatherer's cart.

An incident in October reflected the change in the government's alertness. For contravening the order forbidding relations and friends to accompany corpses to the graveside, eleven persons were committed to Newgate. They were trumpeters, and they had attended at night with trumpets and swords the funeral of a fellow-musician, Samuel Underhill, at Shoreditch.

Fr. Morse observed the regulations concerning the burial of the dead. Except on occasion when people fell suddenly dead in the streets, the 'bearers' of the dead were to be seen only at night. Unaccompanied they carried the swollen and sore-infested corpses, first on boards, and later, when the number of deaths increased, in carts. Passing from street to street they summoned the bereaved with a bell. The dead were dragged out, often from a cellar, where they had been neighbour to the living. The cemeteries were soon filled, and special plague pits were dug in any field or waste land available in the parish or its outskirts. It was an anonymous and impersonal committal, and the poor resented it. Even blessed ground was denied them, for the Bishop of London refused to consecrate any land that would not be used in perpetuity for burial. But when death approached, despair made the poor callous of the fate of their bodies.

In a measure greater than any other attendants on the sick, Morse was able to comfort the dying. Since Catholics were not permitted their own burial ground, it had long been the custom for priests to hold their funeral service in secret, sprinkling some fragments of blessed earth into the open coffin, before it was carried out for burial in the Protestant cemetery. This Morse did at night. The relatives then awaited the bell that announced the coming of the buriers' cart. For the most part the corpses were uncoffined, but the law spared the people the harrowing sight of a communal interment.

On arrival in the fields, the carts tipped their load of dead into the freshly opened pits. Burials in the city cemeteries had ceased in May when the College of Physicians, alarmed at the steady increase of the plague, had called the notice of the Council to the practice of digging up partly decomposed bodies to make room for new victims. The pest-houses had their own arrangements. Within the enclosing palings a rough pit was marked out; and no sooner had a corpse been laid there than some plague-stricken poor man or woman occupied the vacated bed in the nearby timber shed. The same men of the parish were engaged at seven shillings a week to carry the sick to the pest-house and the corpses to the pit. The burier received half as much again.

Through love of pomp and display at funerals many of the poor concealed the cause of death when it was from the plague. This and other practices make any estimate of the number of plague deaths in this or the later outbreak uncertain. The parish bills of mortality are no guide. Although in the first week of October—the week in which Morse published his appeal to Catholics—921 plague deaths were reported, and the official total for the month was 2,626, the actual figure was probably more than double. In the first place, the official returns took no account of mortality among Catholics who, like the Anabaptists and other nonconformists, declined to notify plague deaths to the warden of a Church with which they had nothing in common. Frequently to conceal their harsh treatment, the sick-nurses presented the dead to the parish as non-plague cases; they knew that by wrapping the bodies in wet cloths they could drive inwards the spots and remove all symptoms of the plague. But principally it was the relatives who concealed the cause of death, for they were fearful of being shut up. They were firmly set in their habits. No danger of infection deterred them from calling on the houses of their friends. 'There is a strange opinion here [in London] among the poor', wrote one observer during this plague; 'they hold it a matter of conscience to visit their neighbours in any sickness, yea, though they know it to be infection; even the red cross does not keep them out.' As long as death could be attributed to some other cause or there was any doubt whatsoever that the cause was plague, it was not entered in the weekly plague returns. There were a dozen reasons why the plague should be concealed. Bills of mortality reveal only roughly the increase and decline of the plague; they are no guide to the number of deaths.

In many instances Morse's work was made more difficult by the refusal of his people to receive the sacraments. There is the case, for example, of an old woman in Westminster. For many months she had the plague in a mild form, but she was too aged to recover in the conditions of poverty in which she lived. Fr. Southworth had long tried to persuade her to confess, but had failed up to the time of his arrest. Then Morse visited her along with the other sick whom Southworth had attended. 'With words of comfort and kindness,' he told her the danger she was in, and she confessed. But her servant now caught the plague. She was more obdurate. Morse called on her daily; he stayed with her as death approached, and nursed her in the last violent convulsions that shook her struggling stricken body; 'by alarm and persuasion, it seemed by main force, and at the very second of death, he dragged her back into the sheepfold of Christ'.

Unable to pay for a nurse, the poor Catholic families depended on Morse for medical attention. Although the Catholic doctors worked tirelessly and regardless of the creed of their patients, still, in the autumn and early winter, the sick were too numerous for their attention. Often it fell to Morse to dress their sores, to support in bed dying women in danger of strangling or choking, and hear their faintly spoken confessions as their infectious breath fell across his face. Frequently he would sit with them while they passed into their delirium and death agony, then close their eyes and mouth left open by death, lay out the body, and bless it before burial. Sometimes a heavy sleep mercifully preceded death, but delirium was more common. In their last hours many would break out in extravagant rage and strike in madness at their friends until death ended their ravings. Others shivered and trembled hideously. In their dreams men were known to cry out that they were all on fire. Those that woke again told how they had been among the graves in the churchyard or had fallen alive from some high place into a pest-pit. Cuthbert Holland's household was one frequently visited by Morse. Throughout the winter they were shut in. Morse watched while six of them died of the plague.

Since nurses were engaged by the parish, Morse seldom met them in Catholic households. But in tenements where Catholics and Protestants were shut up together, they often obstructed him in his work. Attendants rather than nurses, they were drawn from the scourings of the womenfolk, and undertook the risks of their work in desperation or want, when the sealing of the city deprived them of all other means of livelihood. They were, of course, illiterate, and apart from a few midwives who now served as attendants, were wholly without skill. Any woman in need of money was accepted by the parish for a weekly wage of five to seven shillings. Often they were known to be criminal or abandoned women. For them the plague was an opportunity of plunder. They entered the shut-up houses with authority—the sick could not eject them—and as a class it was said that they were feared more than the plague itself. Without exaggeration, Dr. Hodges wrote that sometimes 'out of greediness to plunder the dead, they would strangle their patients and charge it to the distemper in their throats. Others would secretly convey the pestilential taint from sores of the infected to those that were well.' In the great plague of 1665 preachers made them the subject of their invective and saw divine vengeance in the case of a nurse who was struck down on the doorstep as she was leaving, 'laden with robberies', a house where all the inmates were dead of the plague. With good grounds they were often suspected of hastening death by administering cold draughts to the sick.

It was a nurse attendant, Mrs. Frances Hall, who was responsible for Morse's first arrest early in November. The woman was employed by an old sick couple, Richard and Mary Seares, who were both Protestants and attended the parish church of St. Giles-in-the-Fields, served throughout the plague by William Haywood, the rector. As she drew near death, Mrs. Seares sent a messenger to her Catholic neighbour, Mrs. Freshwater, who had been visited regularly by Morse since she first fell sick. Morse hurried to see her, and received her and her husband into the Church before they died. But as soon as they had been taken out to burial, the nurse, anxious to gain the statutory reward for informing on a priest, made trouble with William Haywood. She claimed that she had entered the sick-room and found Morse bending over Mary Seares's bed listening to her confession. Moreover, her patient had told her this was what Morse was doing. The local justice was informed. The next day, as Morse was about to enter a house in the parish to give Holy Communion to a dying Catholic, he was stopped by a constable. Ordered to follow him, he was led to the constable's house and there imprisoned. The priest's first concern was for the Blessed Sacrament, which at the time of his arrest he was carrying in a pyx about his neck. 'There in the constable's room he consumed the Blessed Sacrament to prevent it falling into the hands of the heretics, and hid the pyx in a corner. He then summoned the constable, and put some cash into his hands to persuade the man to see that he was released quickly. That same evening he was summoned for examination before the justices of the peace. As he passed along the streets he commended himself and his cause to the Blessed Virgin. All that happened was that he was asked a few perfunctory questions. Was he a priest? Did he enter infected houses? Did he celebrate Mass? At once Morse realised the justices of the peace were irritated that the law had been invoked against him. He answered politely and correctly. Evading the issue of his priesthood, he confessed that he distributed alms he received for the plague-stricken, and that he was acting on behalf of the Queen, who provided the greater part of them. It was true also that he entered infected houses, but openly and in the sight of everyone about. As for saying Mass—he was arrested in the afternoon—no priest offered Mass after mid-day. The magistrate answered: 'We are all aware the Catholics of London are more generous to their sick than we Protestants.' He praised Morse's work and dismissed him. He had been under arrest for half a day. Placing a gold sovereign in the constable's hand, Morse returned with him to his house, gathered his pyx, and completed the call he had been prevented from making. Impressed with Morse's charity, the constable, who later contracted the plague, sought out Morse to instruct him in his faith so that he might die a Catholic.

It is recorded that in the month in which Morse was arrested and set at large again, four hundred and eighty Catholic families were infected, perhaps between two and three thousand persons. In the circumstances Morse could only hand over for instruction to other priests all the poor people who sought to be received into the Church. The number of his converts grew as his name became great for kindness. But also his

difficulties increased. In London, particularly in time of
plague, there were always men who could obtain a livelihood
by claiming the reward for 'informing' on priests. Owing to
Morse's success in making converts, they could now rely on
the support of clergymen, like Mr. White of Westminster, who
had secured the imprisonment of Fr. Southworth. Nor was it
ever difficult to stir up the latent frenzy of the Londoners
against Catholics. Within a month of Morse's arrest a petition
was presented to the Council by the parishioners of St. Giles-
in-the-Fields. 'Humbly', they deplored the 'miserable state
they were in by the great increase of those of the Romish
Church in the parish, where they are so exceedingly multiply-
ing daily that in that part called Bloomsbury there are as many
or more than the Protestants.'

Among the Catholics Morse attended during November
there was a youth who lodged in the same tenement as a young
Protestant woman. The plague took a slow course with him,
but eventually he died. Morse then warned the woman of the
danger she was in from the plague. 'He spoke to her of eternal
things' and the girl was so 'deeply moved that she asked for
instruction in the faith'. The plague was still in the house. On
the day arranged for her reception into the Church—it was
agreed that it should be done at night—Morse was unable to
visit her 'because of the large number of the dying he had to
attend'. He agreed to go the following day. Meanwhile word
of the girl's intention had got abroad among her neighbours.
Throughout the day two constables stood guard in front of the
door. At evening Morse appeared in the street. The girl, who
had been watching for the priest's approach, signalled the
danger from behind the garden wall of her shut-in house.
Morse failed to see her. Just at the moment he came up to the
door the two constables drew away in the opposite direction
to take their evening meal. There and then over the wall

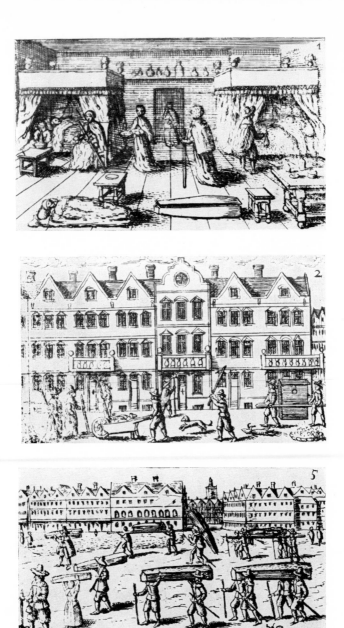

PLAGUE SCENES
See Appendix A.

PLAGUE SCENES
See Appendix A.

Morse hastily completed her instruction, heard her confession and received her into the Church.

It was a young Catholic that on one occasion took Morse to the pest-house in St. Giles-in-the-Fields. The man had contracted a bigamous marriage. 'Every natural instinct' in the priest 'revolted against the scene', so loathsome were his condition and surroundings. Sitting on the edge of the filthy bed, Morse heard his confession, 'compelled to hold his ear close to the man's lips lest he should be overheard'. The account goes on: 'But God in his goodness at once repaid the Father for this act of self-denial, for a great light was given to the sick young man to see the heinousness of his sins, so much so that the words of his confession were almost choked by his tears and sobs.' Morse had 'lavished upon him every token of kindness in order to excite in his penitent the hope of pardon', and now, when he heard him express his contrition, the priest feared the man might die, so vehement did he become. His wife, too, was brought back to the Church, before Morse visited the man in the pest-house for the last time to give him the final anointing on his plague-spotted ears, lips and forehead.

In December severe frosts set in. On the seventh of the month George Lowe, writing to the Earl of Middlesex, expressed a hope that the 'hard weather will abate the plague'. It was noticeable that it was already on the decline, but there was no certainty it might not touch another peak before it was over.

Shortly after Christmas Morse once again was briefly interrupted in his work. Coming out of a visited house after nightfall, he was suddenly arrested. Looking hard into his captor's face, he recognised him as the pursuivant John Cook. He had 'to think quickly. There was a chance he might be able to bribe the man. Without hesitating he placed in his hands 'the small sum in cash' he happened to have in his pocket. It was accepted but the man proposed that Morse should come back at once and pay him a larger sum for perpetual immunity from his attentions. Morse hesitated to comply. 'He did not think it wise to agree, for he knew how little faith could be given to this kind of man, and he knew too that they were out merely for money.' He was again free.

12

AT THE SIGN OF THE SUN

By the statute of 1606 'to prevent and avoid dangers which may grow by Popish recusants', a reward was given to any person who laid information leading to the arrest of a priest for saying Mass or performing any priestly function. The reward amounted to a third of the forfeitures suffered by the Catholics assisting at the Mass, provided this did not total more than fifty pounds. The statute made priest-catching a lucrative occupation.

During the eleven years (1629–40) in which Charles I ruled without Parliament, this law was largely in abeyance. But it remained on the statute book and had already brought into existence companies, or rather gangs of informers, furnished with warrants issued by sheriffs or justices of the peace in the days of the last Parliament. Although they received no encouragement from the government or local authorities, nevertheless their warrant gave power to search houses for evidence of priestly activity and to deliver priests or lay persons into the hands of the justices of the peace. When this was done the magistrates were compelled to take notice. Frequently, however, the pursuivants found it more profitable to offer a priest freedom for an agreed sum. It was a form of blackmail that could be gone through any number of times, so that the accumulated ransoms amounted often to a larger sum than the percentage of the forfeitures that could be claimed. Under cover of these dormant warrants, and in the name of law, 'outrages, abuses, and misdemeanours' were committed: goods, plate and jewels, in no way connected with the altar, were taken on the plea that they were the 'goods of Jesuits'. The members of the company would exchange or sell information and share profits, and a priest no sooner purchased immunity from one member than he found himself under arrest by another. The law gave the priests no protection; it was more prudent for them to submit. In prison they would have to bear the extortion of their keepers; even on a financial calculation it was wiser to bribe off the professional priest-catcher.

Leader of the principal company of priest-catchers was Francis Newton. Insistently he styled himself, simply, 'a gentleman'. More correctly Morse referred to him as 'a man of infamous life and behaviour', and from information given by his friends among the London lawyers, was able to expose the 'dishonest practices' which had led to his public disgrace and expulsion from the profession of attorney-at-law. This was in 1627. In the same year he took up the occupation of pursuivant and obtained his warrant for the 'apprehension of Jesuits, seminary priests and transporters of children overseas'. In this new livelihood he caused as much trouble to the Ministers of Charles I as to priests themselves. During the next ten years he claimed to have brought before Secretary Coke and others, 'at his great charge and hazard of life', as many as thirty-seven priests. These, in due course, were all discharged, and in return for their services both Newton and Cook were several times committed to prison.

If William Prynne is to be believed, Francis Newton, before taking a penny from Fr. Morse, had amassed more than eight watches seized from priests, 'two rich suits of vestments', which the Queen bought back for two hundred pounds with some other possessions that the company had pawned. Apart from Cook there were other notable members in the firm. Thomas Mayo, a renegade priest, was a valued 'purveyor of priests' movements', and kept a constant watch on the Jesuit rest-house at Cheam, which was nominally the property of a gentleman, Bartholomew Freeman. On one occasion Mayo presented himself there to arrest the Superior on the day before seven priests were due to arrive for a triduum of prayer. It was about the time that Morse stayed in the house to prepare himself by prayer for his work among the plague-stricken.

In the same company with Newton and Mayo were Gray, Wadsworth and Lloyd. They pursued Morse with increasing persistence. They were present at his trial. They brought about first his condemnation and then, after his first reprieve, his death.

With cunning Newton chose the moment for his first move, when he was certain of some measure of popular support.

Lying sick in the parish pest-house was a retired pirate captain, a Calvinist and octogenarian. 'Credited with every kind of crime and violent in his loathing of the name of God,' he was visited there by Morse. He confessed his sins, received baptism and, as Alegambe says, 'was piloted into the port of heaven'. The man's Calvinist relatives were enraged—he had been a preacher before he became a pirate. Morse had arranged for his Catholic burial, but at the last moment they fought to extricate his corpse from the pile of dead: only a sudden uproar among the bystanders prevented it. The incident was quickly over; nevertheless it gave Newton the opportunity he sought. From that moment, says Alegambe, the fanatics pursued Morse with even greater venom.

Some days later, 'as I was returning from the bedside of a plague-sick woman who was lying in a most critical condition', wrote Morse, 'I was unexpectedly assailed by two pursuivants, John Cook and Francis Newton'.

It was Monday, 27 February. Newton and Cook 'were returning out of London through Holborn'. Newton had not previously known Morse, but Cook recognised him without difficulty: he had arrested and released him only a few weeks earlier. By prearrangement, as the account says, 'Cook wished Newton to attack Morse as a supposed priest, which he did accordingly.' Behind them stood John Thompson, an attorney of the King's Bench, who dwelt in Tuttle Street. He had been persuaded to be present merely to give the appearance of greater authority to their action. Morse was unimpressed. He demanded to see their warrant, but 'they jeered at me in reply, and threatened to handcuff me, and this went on until we reached a tavern in Fetter Lane. Here at last they produced the warrant giving them authority. It had been issued as far back as 1632. I declared it was worthless and outdated. Then all of them became half intoxicated. In an attempt to recover my liberty I offered them a sum of money—it was smaller than they had agreed amongst themselves—and they rejected it.' Presumably it was all he carried on his person. 'At this', says Morse, 'they pretended they wanted to take me to one of the King's Secretaries for examination, so they put me in a boat and ferried me up-river to Westminster. All the way there Newton was pouring out a stream of curses, saying blasphemously that he wanted to see whether the saints I honoured would come to my aid and deliver me from their hands.' They disembarked at Westminster and Newton led the way to another inn in the Broad Sanctuary kept by John Spencer. 'Here', says Morse, 'they immediately searched me to the skin, but they found only some keys with a medal of St. Ignatius and St. Francis Xavier', whose canonisation he had witnessed as a student in Rome. 'These they took from me and afterwards produced in court.'

It was against the plague regulations for an innkeeper to

receive any guest that had been in contact with the plague-stricken. Not only had Morse, less than an hour earlier, been seen to come out of an infected house; he himself had been taken with the plague, and, as he remarked, the 'sores on my body were scarcely healed'. That night, by the direction of Newton, no one was allowed to speak with Morse.

It was doubtless Newton's fear that he himself would be prosecuted for contravening the plague regulations that accounted for his strange behaviour the following morning.

'On the following day', Morse's narrative continues, 'Cook returned to offer me in his name and Newton's a financial proposition for my release. While we were discussing it, my servant arrived at the inn door. He had been wondering why I had not returned home, and was afraid that while I was visiting the sick at night I might have been stabbed in the back by assassins or (as proved the case) captured by pursuivants. He had taken another man as companion and had searched for me everywhere. Just at the right moment he had arrived at the inn where I was kept prisoner. He was not allowed to see me, but I recognised his voice, showed myself and, in the hearing of all, asked him to take steps to see that the Queen was informed as soon as possible about the place where I was held. My only purpose in speaking like this was to put myself in a position to bargain for my liberty at a smaller price. But my servant seriously believed that I had asked him to do just what I said, and he took up the matter with great energy. Through the intercession of a friend he obtained from the Queen's confessor a promise that he would petition for my immediate release: but only one thing he required—that some member of the Society should be sent to give the confessor a detailed confirmation of the events just as they had occurred.' He asked this because he wished to obtain a more authoritative statement. The confessor may have thought it difficult to approach the Queen merely on the statement of a serving-man.

All that day Morse remained confined at the inn in the Broad Sanctuary. He was given no food and feared that if his detention lasted any longer his health would not endure the strain, 'for I had barely recovered', he says, 'from the plague. Moreover, the sick would suffer severely, for they were helpless and dependent on me alone.' It was imperative to strike a bargain at once.

'After much debating and many conferences between us all that day,'—this is Cook's account, given after he had broken with Newton, and it confirms with greater precision Morse's own journal—'the conclusion and bargain was that Mr. Morse should give Newton five pounds, and so be discharged and set at liberty. The conditions that Mr. Newton required were that Mr. Morse should promise not to acquaint anyone with what he gave for his liberty; secondly, that if the Lords of the Council should have notice of the arrest and call for him, he should again render himself prisoner to him.'

On these terms an agreement was negotiated by Cook. Newton approved; he had been unwilling to treat directly with Morse 'for fear of being questioned for it', as he told Cook.

The evening of the same day Newton, taking Cook and Spencer, conducted Morse to the Sun Tavern in Westminster. Over a pint of sack, ordered by Newton at Morse's expense, the execution of the agreement was discussed. Spencer was not taken into Newton's confidence. Cook entertained him apart.

When the conference ended, Cook was ordered to take Morse to the Strand. There, from some Catholic friends, the priest was 'to procure the said five pounds'; this done, he was to be set free. If the money could not be got immediately—it was already nine o'clock in the evening—Morse was to be allowed 'to go among his friends' after giving his word to surrender himself again the next day if he was still unable to collect his ransom.

Morse paid for the sack, then with Cook left for the Strand. The rest of the party stayed on at the Sun 'drinking up the wine that remained. And in that time Newton further told Spencer that Mr. Morse was a weakly and sickly man and he had given him leave to go to a doctor or an apothecary and he would return the same night or the next day.'

Clearly Newton was embarrassed; he feared also that Morse might die on his hands.

'It was night and the hour ill-suited for disturbing friends,' continues Morse, 'and their plans went awry.' The apothecary in the Strand was not at home, so, still in Cook's company, he walked over the fields to Holborn and there knocked at the door of a Catholic cutler named William Hodson, 'acquainting him with the present use he had of five pounds to redeem him from his restraint'. Hodson made no difficulty. He had the five pounds at hand, and invited Cook to a tavern near-by where he promised to pay him over a pint of wine.

The cutler thought again. In his house were two Catholic gentlemen. On the plea of borrowing the ransom money from them, he went upstairs and made his plans. 'Understanding the matter', writes Morse, 'they all seized their swords of a sudden and leapt out into the street. There and then they would have pursued the man to his death (for he had taken instantly to his heels) if I had not made every effort and entreaty to calm them and succeeded finally in turning them from their precipitate purpose.'[1] It was the night of 28 February

[1] The magistrates' report is less vivid: 'Cook, espying the gentlemen,' it states, 'made haste away, leaving Mr. Morse in the street without wishing or requiring him to return back with him, or calling any officer or other person in any sort to apprehend or stay the said Mr. Morse. Nor did Newton or Cook that night or the next day either search or at all endeavour to attack Mr. Morse, but (as it seemeth) relied on his agreement

1638. Morse was again a free man in the plague-stricken city.

By the terms of the agreement made at the Sun, Morse had bound himself to surrender the next day if he failed to deliver his ransom. It was an agreement made under duress and with a dishonest intent. It is unlikely that Morse considered that it bound him. He had more than discharged any debt by his intercession on behalf of Cook's life. Still, for the sake of securing immunity from further molestation, he proposed to hand over the money. For twenty-four hours now his sick people had been without assistance; he was impatient to return to them.

But the intervention of his servant forced him to alter his plans. 'The next day', Morse explains, 'my man happened by total chance to meet in the street his friend, the same person he had asked only the previous day to assist him in approaching the Queen with the purpose of obtaining my release. This man had just heard of my escape. He protested that my behaviour seemed most unworthy of me and most uncomplimentary to the Queen, in so much as I had begged her help and had such little confidence in obtaining it that I had taken things into my own hands and purchased my liberty.' With his sensitive courtesy Morse 'weighed the matter over'. Then his account continues, 'I decided to escape the dilemma by placing myself again in the hands of the pursuivants, as I had undertaken to do if I did not obtain the ransom demanded.'

During his day of liberty Morse entrusted his work to his fellow-Jesuit, Fr. Edward Lusher. Late that evening he returned to the Sun, where Newton 'received ill' the news of the Queen's intervention. Momentarily Morse had outplayed him; but Newton's resource was greater. Morse tells the story.

---

or promise to pay the five pounds or to render himself a prisoner to Newton again.'

'The next day, in order to counter the Queen's request and forestall the King's clemency, Newton approached the King's Secretary [Sir John Coke]. He was a man who had a lifelong hostility to Catholics. Newton set his business before him and returned not merely with a commendation for the work he had done, but with a promise of a large reward and with a warrant also to examine my moral character and conduct. Moreover, he was not on any account to set me free, even at the Queen's bidding, unless he was first shown a written order for my release.'

Morse was detained at the Sun. There, two days later, he was visited by a 'person of rank'. Reassured now by Coke, Newton became truculent and detained Morse's visitor on a charge of high treason 'until the man had proved that he was out on parole and was, moreover, protected by the rights of a foreign state'. Morse does not give the name of his friend, but he was able to speak to him apart and explain how he had been constrained to hand himself back to his captors. When the man left, Newton, 'suspecting that he might perchance have brought me something, again searched all my pockets and carefully shook my clothes in case anything should be concealed in them.'

As the days passed Newton strengthened his grasp. Lent had begun. It was Morse's first experience of captivity in a private establishment. He resumed the ordered life he had set himself in York Castle. 'During this time I behaved as though I were in a secluded prison. I had to endure many insults and much ill-treatment because I insisted on having nothing to do with all the people who came and went, but passed those holy days of Lent in fasting and in prayer.'

13

OLD BAILEY

WITHIN a few hours of his interview with Sir John Coke, the King's Secretary, on 2 March, Francis Newton was busy preparing a case for the prosecution of Henry Morse. No priest had been executed for nearly ten years. But Newton was determined now to make good all his failures to secure the hanging of a priest. With an experience and zest inspired by long frustration, he set about his task. Fortune at first was with him. 'On the fifth of this month', writes Morse, 'I was brought before the Privy Council. I was charged with persuading many persons from the Protestant religion and reconciling them to the Catholic Church.' By chance, the same day William Haywood, the Rector of St. Giles-in-the-Fields, presented a complaint to the Council, signed by himself, the three churchwardens, and William Hyde, the parish constable. In distress at the 'great increase' of Catholics they begged the Council 'for the glory of God and the suppressing of this great enormity' to take measures for a 'reformation'. Newton's deposition was more detailed: it listed more than eighteen persons, including Robert Webb, a former constable, and his wife, who were prepared to give testimony of Morse's perversive activity.

The two petitions, laid separately and on the same day before the Council, made Morse's immediate release impossible.

At once an inquiry was ordered into the alleged complaints. For the next twenty days Newton was occupied in preparing his evidence. Meanwhile Morse remained his private prisoner, 'in complete solitary confinement' at the Sun.

'On the twenty-sixth day of March, however,' continues Morse, 'a warrant was issued from his Majesty's Privy Council and signed by twelve Councillors, whereby I was ordered to remove from the inn at Westminster to the prison of Newgate. This was done on the twenty-eighth.' The meeting was held at Whitehall, and was attended by Laud, whose signature appears first on the warrant addressed to the keeper of Newgate, requiring him to keep Morse a 'safe prisoner' in his charge until he received further orders from the board.

It was seven years since Morse had been released from York Castle: he had spent four years there, and, earlier, four in the New prison. It was his first experience of Newgate. The impressions of the newcomer were set down by another writer who, on passing the huge, barred wooden gates, found himself in the prison lodge 'encompassed by a parcel of ill-looking fellows who eyed me as if they would examine every part of me from head to foot; not as tailors to take measure of me, but as footpads that survey the goodness of the clothes first, before they grow intimate with the linings'. Unlike other prisons, Newgate had changed little since the early days of Elizabeth. In the month of Morse's transfer there from the Sun more than forty-seven criminals condemned to the gallows had been given a temporary reprieve owing to the plague, for large crowds were certain to gather for an execution. Already in April the previous year the gaol had become overcrowded; soon afterwards it was reported to be a breeding-place for the plague. But to release the prisoners would increase lawlessness in the city; transportation was impracticable 'for none durst carry them abroad', and it was thought that to dispose of them

by hanging in cold blood was 'hard'. The stench of one poor
prisoner alone was suffocating. But there they remained, sick
and half-starved, when Morse joined them on 28 March. His
privacy was at an end. Even at meals his feelings revolted, for
at table, as a versifier wrote,

> When everyone has got his snack
> Some hungry souls with scarce a rug on
> Cut, slash, eat like hungry dragon
> And grease themselves from jaw to groin
> For napkins are as scarce as coin.

As no executions were carried out for fear of the plague,
Morse was spared perhaps the worst sight of Newgate life.
For on the eve of his hanging it was the custom for the criminal
to make friends with his executioner, who without charge
allowed him the freedom of his kitchen to make merry and 'to
whore and bitch in'.

It was still Lent. Morse continued his order of prayer and
fasting. 'Then after a few days', he writes, 'Newton and Cook
interrupted me in my devotions. With vehemence they
pressed me, in consideration of their labour, to pay them, on an
alleged order of the Council, a fee of ten pounds sterling.'
Morse refused to parley, though, as he said, 'they threatened
me should I disobey with still more barbarous treatment. But
I continued to answer firmly. I said that the way I had been
handled up to the present time had been so outrageous that
henceforth I should neither expect good from them nor fear
harm.' With that the episode was closed.

The next twenty-five days passed without incident. In that
'ancient repository of living bodies', as one inmate called it,
Morse's health grew worse. Up three pairs of stairs, he lived
in a large room entered through the prison chapel. Here, with
other 'gentlemen' prisoners, he continued his devotions

through Holy Week and the season beyond. 'The bars of the windows were as thick as the wrist, and the chamber walls, made entirely of stone, were bedaubed with texts of Scripture, scribbled in charcoal, and with scraps of verses composed according to the disposition and circumstances of the several tenants thereof. As for beds, there were steads for three to be laid upon, made of boards, but neither flocks nor feathers enough in all to make one. The tables and chairs were of like antiquity and use.' Compared with the conditions in the cellars on the other side of the gateway, living was comfortable. Frequently the conversation of the older inmates turned on the last hours of criminals in the gaol and their dying speeches: they were gone over time and again with melancholy and affectionate admiration. It had always been so, and so it continued for many decades to come. Indeed, the humour and rough-spokenness of many common thieves when they came to the scaffold never deserted them. John Biggs, a later felon, was typical of them all. Hanged at Tyburn for robbery, he addressed the crowd: 'Men, women and children, I am come hither to hang like a pendulum for endeavouring to be rich too soon.' Then, urged by the Protestant minister to confess more crimes than he had committed, he added: 'I never was a murderer, unless killing fleas and such little harmless cruelties fall under the statute; neither can I charge myself with being a whore-master, since the female gentry had always the ascendancy over me, not I over them.' With no 'whining and crying' he died professing himself a 'true blue wholesale Protestant'.

As he had done in York Castle, Morse again moved among the criminals of all classes, taking care only that he was not seen administering the sacraments, for until he had been convicted for receiving orders beyond the seas, he was forced to observe the caution practised by his brethren outside. His

work was made easy by the worthlessness of the men who held
the post of official chaplain at Newgate: 'their characters were
as low as their salaries', and their salaries they augmented by
publishing the last confessions of condemned felons. 'Orthodox Sam', as he was known—he held the post later in the century—was more regular in his duties than his predecessors,
who merely visited the gaol after each assize. Sam, however,
preached to his flock on every occasion, 'a very Tertullian in
respect of some of his predecessors', who customarily divided
criminals into three classes, 'Sabbath-breakers, drunkards and
whore-masters'. Although Morse fell into none of these cate-
gories, the rough classification was correct. It was at evening
that Morse could move more freely. Then also visitors flocked
to the prison, carrying liquor to comfort the inmates; and both
upstairs and in the cellars below Morse's companions 'plied
their glasses very furiously' until the gaoler dispersed the company for the night.

The keeper at Newgate exercised an unrestricted jurisdiction. As at York his office was purchased, and on one occasion
was known to have changed hands at a fee of three thousand
five hundred pounds. For every favour or comfort payment
was exacted. To obtain temporary release from his irons, any
common house-breaker had to pay the keeper. A scale of
charges existed whereby he might 'purchase a sleeping hole a
little free of vermin . . . or wholesome air enough to keep the
lungs from being choked up'. Since these amenities were
beyond the pockets of the poorer prisoners, the money was
'supplied by his jades or brother-rogues abroad, who must rob
or whore to support him even with the common necessities of
life'. But this was but one example of the old verse-maker's
complaint that

> Justice with the gaoler's trade
> In every point goes retrograde.

For four weeks Morse remained in Newgate before he received intimation of his forthcoming trial. 'On the twenty-first day of April I was told to get ready to stand my trial at the Old Bailey. But that day I did not obtain a hearing.'

The next day, 'the twenty-second of April, the gaoler again led me to the same building where the Judges and a large number of people had foregathered. The sepulchral voice of the usher summoned me before the Bench. I was ordered to raise my hand in the customary fashion.' Then the trial began. It appears to have lasted the greater part of the day. Morse records the incidents in the exact phrasing of the trained lawyer. As a Catholic he was allowed no counsel for defence; but he himself argued forcefully his own case for acquittal.

'The two counts of the indictment were read out. The first, that by authority derived from the Roman See I had been ordained priest contrary to the laws of the realm. The second, that I had seduced his Majesty's subjects from their due faith and allegiance. On both counts I replied to the question "guilty or not guilty?" that I was in no manner guilty and, following the custom of the court, I entrusted my case to God and to the country.

'The evidence was then called, and I was ordered to draw closer so that I could be heard without difficulty. From the opposite side of the court the witnesses appeared. Among them were two pursuivants, Newton and Gray, both most wicked men. With them was a watchman named Pope and somebody I did not know called Bailey; also three women of the lower class, Maderson and Hall, with another from Westminster.

'Then in a clear and fearless voice Newton swore that I was a priest and had once confessed the fact to him in a way that left no doubt about it. He said that when he had asked me whether I was a Jesuit, I had denied it; but that when he had pressed me to say whether or not I was a priest, I had not denied it. In most strong terms I protested against this statement, and said that no trust whatsoever should be placed in the word of such a notorious rogue.

' "That is true," answered the presiding Judge. "He may may be a rogue. Still, it is possible for you to be hanged on his testimony."

'And he added, "Now what have you to say? Are you a priest?"

'I answered that I was unworthy of that office. He put the question to me again. I answered:

' "Your Lordship, I am utterly unworthy of the office."

' "But," said the Judge, "there are men who can be priests and nevertheless unworthy. Swear, then, on the word of a priest that you are not one."

' "But," I replied, "the laws of the realm do not permit an oath to be demanded of the accused person." '

It was the reply he had made to the aldermen of Newcastle. Then his priesthood remained unproven and he had been released. Secretly he prayed, perhaps, that the same defence would again baffle the Bench. The Judge persisted.

' "If you refuse the oath," he said, "it is clear that you are guilty."

' "Be that as it may," I answered, "but it is clear that it is no proof whatever." '

Morse's emphatic and exact reply impressed the Judge. Immediately he sought other grounds for conviction. Morse continues:

'Then this Judge, turning to another point, stated that it was as a priest that I had been committed to prison by his Majesty's Council.

' "That proves nothing," I retorted, "except that credit was given far too readily to Newton's assertions."

'Then once again the same Judge asked me whether I was a priest, and I persisted in the same reply.

' "But this very fact, that while you emphatically deny everything else, you quibble on this one point, makes it clear that you are a priest."

' "Assuredly that is no proof," I answered.

'At this Newton broke in, saying that he had understood from three Popish priests that I was a Jesuit, and that one of them had spoken of me in terms of disdain. He added that I was a most dangerous man and a "consultor" among the Jesuits, and on this account he had been especially enjoined by Canterbury—that is how they refer to the Archbishop—to arrest me and, after my arrest, to guard me with the greatest care, if he valued his own life.

'The woman Maderson was then called. She asserted that I had anointed a certain woman, using some kind of red cloth which hung round my neck. I answered her: "I had applied to the woman," I said, "a medicament which I carried in a small bag made of purple cloth." This started a discussion among the Judges as to whether the point was relevant or not. Then one of them asked me in all seriousness, demanding a direct answer—was it or was it not holy water? I answered, No.

'Gray then stated that he had seen a man on bended knees making a sacramental confession to me; and Hall then came forward and said he had once heard a dying woman distinctly admit she had confessed to me.

'When these witnesses had finished, I was asked whether I was a Catholic. I admitted that I was.

' "A Roman Catholic?" the Judge asked.

' "Of course," I said, "a Roman Catholic. What other kind of Catholic can there be?" '

Morse was never a man easily to conceal his irritation. His

outburst was understood by another Judge on the Bench. Morse gives his name simply as Jones.

Sir William Jones, a Carnarvonshire man, belonged to the same generation as Morse's father, and had perhaps known him when he left St. Edmund's Hall, Oxford, to enter Furnivall's Inn. He was Lent reader at Lincoln's Inn during Morse's last year as a law student. For five years he had been Chief Justice in Ireland, then a Judge of Common Pleas. Municipal legislation was his favourite study, and this interest and his residence in Holborn might have made him familiar with Morse's work. His intervention at this moment of the trial was courageous.

'One of the other Judges,' writes Morse, 'rising from his seat denied that I was guilty under the statute of persuasions. Whatever I had done in the name of religion, I had not in any interpretation done with the intent of alienating the King's subjects from their allegiance. To this the other Judges promptly assented.

'Then the presiding Judge asked me whether I had anything further to adduce in my defence. This is a summary of what I answered:

' "The evidence against me has no weight whatever. The woman Hall has spoken in utter ignorance of all that confession means. I did indeed persuade a dying woman to examine her conscience and helped her to do this, so that she might have less difficulty in expressing sorrow for her sins."

'At this the presiding Judge interposed.

' "And who, pray, authorised you to perform that task?"

'I answered: "Each and all of us are authorised to assist our neighbour in need of this kind." '

Morse continued: ' "As for Gray's evidence concerning the man whom he alleges to have seen kneeling close at my feet, these are the facts. He was a gentleman and preferred that posture to any other because it gave him greater relief from the pain he was then suffering. Whether or not he was making his confession, there is no possible means of Gray knowing, since confession is always a matter of the strictest secrecy. And for these reasons no witness has confirmed on oath any of the charges against me—rather they have all cleared me—with the one exception of Newton, a worthless creature of no credit, who on a previous occasion was dismissed from the courts in disgrace." In support of this statement I gave the names of the Judges present there in court who were cognisant of the facts, and I added confirmation from what many persons had said and was, in fact, common report.

'Then I contested the statement to which Newton had sworn, namely, that I once admitted to him, of all people, that I was a priest. It had no foundation whatever. Indeed, what would have induced me to make a rogue, a spy and my bitter personal enemy my confidant, and confess to him something which, by the laws of the realm, I knew to be a capital offence? Besides, I had been at pains to deny that I was a Jesuit—which in the eyes of the law was perhaps a lesser offence and one involving slighter peril. In conclusion I said I would be greatly insulted if my word did not command more credence than his, even backed as it was by his oath.'

It was a strong speech and well argued. Sir William Jones addressing the jury, summed up: 'Gentlemen, notice that this man has been accused of two things. He has been accused of perverting his Majesty's subjects and of being a priest. Of the first, there is not a scrap of real evidence. It is the second charge, therefore, that you must consider.'

The presiding Judge repeated the instruction. The twelve jurymen retired.

'After a very short absence', says Morse, 'they returned to court and without a dissentient voice pronounced me guilty of being a priest, but not guilty on the charge of persuasion.

Whereupon I courteously thanked the presiding Judge, who turned to his brethren on the Bench, and said, "Look, he actually thanks me because he has been found guilty."

' "My Lord," I said, "I thank you deeply and from the bottom of my heart."

'And so the case ended, and I was led back to prison.'

Sentence was not passed that day. Morse had defended himself ably. In his account Morse does not mention the affidavits of the thirteen parishioners of St. Giles-in-the-Fields, each independently testifying either that they did not know him, or, if they did know him, that they had always been Catholics. Their statements, dated 19 April, four days before the trial, may perhaps have been laid before the Bench and accounted for the brave statement of Mr. Justice Jones. 'To my knowledge', testified one parishioner, 'I never saw Mr. Morse in my life, and by such information as I have taken from my servants and others that have lived in my house, I am morally certain that he was never within my house nor in St. Giles' parish while I lived there, nor anywhere else where I kept house.' Similarly, John Green, labourer, Cecily Crowe, a widow eighty years old, and others, all swore that Newton's assertions were false; they had long been Catholics, and they and their families would have perished if they had not been relieved by Mr. Morse.

Present in court was Fr. Matthew Wilson, formerly Jesuit Superior of the London district and now Provincial. The same evening he wrote an account of the trial to Fr. Mutius Vitelleschi, the General of the Society, and informed him at the same time that he proposed immediately to allow Fr. Morse to take his final vows as a Jesuit.

'The next day, Tuesday in Easter week, 23 April,' writes Morse, 'in this very prison I was more closely bound to the Society, making my solemn profession of the three vows of religion before Fr. Edward Lusher.' And in words reminiscent of the concluding pages of Fr. John Gerard's *Autobiography*, he recorded his gratitude for 'this signal and unexpected blessing'[1].

'May God grant that while I live I may never cease to act in a manner worthy of this high honour, which I acknowledge I have done nothing to deserve from His divine hand and providence; and may I bear always in my heart the testimony of my gratitude, and, as long as I live, never cease to give thanks for it, if not by the increase of good works, at least by the desire to accomplish them.'

It was two months before the General's reply reached London. 'Your Reverence did rightly and gave me much pleasure' he wrote; and he thanked Fr. Wilson for sending him a detailed account of the trial.

[1] When the great plague broke out in London twenty-eight years later, Fr. Lusher offered his services to the sick as Morse had done in 1636. He was then in Cheshire. Charles II, who knew him, said perhaps unjustly, that he was quick to ride to London on report of the plague as his own ministers were to ride out of it. He was then in his seventy-seventh year. He died a victim of the infection on 27 September 1665.

ARCHBISHOP LAUD

ON 26 April 1637, the day after Fr. Lusher's visit to Newgate, Morse was summoned to the Old Bailey. 'Sentence was to be passed that day on the other criminals', writes Morse. 'Conflicting forecasts of my fate had been made: some thought that judgment would be passed, others that I would not even be taken before the Bench. Whether it was by error or intent I do not know, but I was, in fact, summoned. And accordingly I set my thoughts on heaven and braced myself with prayer bravely to receive the sentence. But it was not pronounced. Instead the Judge ordered me back to prison, not without certain expressions of honour and respect, for the King had given instructions for my sentence to be deferred. He was indignant because he had been misinformed. He had been led to believe it was certain that if he gave permission for my case to come into court, it would be established by a mass of evidence not only that I was a priest but that I had seduced his subjects from their allegiance to him.'

Nevertheless the verdict stood. Charles I had never wished to prosecute. Soon after Morse's transference to Newgate, a petition had been addressed to the King for Morse's release. Momentarily it was effective, and the King was inclined to waive proceedings against Morse. However, Sir John Coke, Newton's ally on the Council, interposed: he had insisted on a trial and assured the King that Morse was a 'dangerous' subject against whom several treasonable facts could be proved. The King had then yielded.

Morse had done well in face of the determination of Coke to secure his conviction. It is clear that his speech was more forceful than his own precise summary suggests. It was delivered in controlled anger. Its merciless exposure of Newton's true character was never forgotten. Although acquitted on the charge of 'seducing', Morse had been convicted of his priesthood. Newton had partially succeeded. Eight years later he secured a sentence on this previous conviction. Morse was never re-tried.

At the time of writing his prison journal, Morse was unaware that the King had intervened to prevent sentence being passed on him.

As soon as the jury had returned its verdict, a Catholic gentleman present in court had sought out George Con, the papal agent at the Queen's Court. 'The Queen was in bed', reported Con to Rome. 'She had a slight pain in her chest which lasted all that day and the following day. So I awaited the return of the King and represented the matter to his Majesty. He asked me why I had not informed him earlier, and I replied that I wanted his Majesty to learn in an authoritative manner what I had told him in confidence from the beginning, namely, that the Jesuit was guilty of nothing more than being a priest and of administering the sacraments to the plague-stricken.

'The King replied: "Don't trouble yourself. I will find a solution."'

Con had then urged the King to make Morse's arrest an excuse for 'doing away with the pursuivants'; but Charles correctly replied 'that he had no power to do this, for they were the servants of the Bench: but whenever they made a mistake he would have them punished'.

The King was in earnest. Con urged him to start with Newton.

The Queen, who was present, interjected, 'Have him hanged', and she added, with sarcasm, 'and I do not wish to be under the slightest obligation to you for the favour.'

The following evening Con again waited on the King after the meeting of the Council. Leading his suitor out on to the balcony of the Queen's chamber, Charles smilingly greeted the envoy. Already, he informed him, he had summoned to his presence the judge who had presided at Morse's trial and had warned him against proceeding in that way for the future. Then he comforted Con. 'Don't disturb yourself over this, because disorder is sometimes the cause of better order. I have given orders to Windebank to see that sentence is not pronounced against our Jesuit. And I assure you that I do not want bloodshed for the sake of religion.' Con then kissed the King's hand. 'I hope', he said, 'that your Majesty will never have occasion to shed the blood of your Catholic subjects.' He then retired.

Accordingly on 24 April Morse was treated respectfully by the Judges and then led back to Newgate.

During the next month, on the instruction of the Council, an inquiry was held into the behaviour of the pursuivants. Two magistrates, Henry Fuller and Edward Jenner, were appointed to receive the findings. On 27 May their report was laid before the Council. Morse gave evidence in prison. He offered to testify on oath to all the details of his arrest and illegal detention in Spencer's house. But this was unnecessary for Newton's man, John Cook, had already broken with his master and given an affidavit which more than confirmed Morse's deposition. Although, as Cook confessed, he had on his first examination denied everything which he now testified, he had done so from

fear that if he 'manifested the dealings Newton had with
Morse' it might turn out 'very prejudicial and dangerous',
since he was 'Newton's man and his chief and only instrument
in all these proceedings'.

Cook's confession was presented to the King independently
of the magistrates' report on Newton. It had been obtained by
Mr. Philip Roper, a cousin of Fr. Henry More, Blount's successor as Provincial, and from other London Catholics, including, perhaps, the gentleman who had pursued Cook from
the chandler's house in Holborn on the night following Morse's
arrest. The magistrates begged for an examination into the
charge that Newton, after arresting Morse, had proceeded to
strike a bargain for his release; and they demanded 'due
punishment' if he should be found guilty. The moment
seemed favourable for Morse's release. His successful defence
before the Bench had pleased the King, for it had endorsed the
opinion he had maintained against the Council.

Morse, however, lay in Newgate for another month. He
then addressed a personal letter to Charles I. After narrating
briefly the circumstances of his arrest and trial, his acquittal on
the charge of persuasion and his conviction for his priesthood 'on the sole and only testimony of Newton', he begged
the King, who 'out of his clemency and justice had preserved
him from the sentence of death due by law', to free him now
'from death in this prison' of Newgate. With the plague still
'thereabouts, his sickness and weakness is increased and his life
endangered': he was, in fact, near death. Still weak from the
plague when he was first captured, for four months he had
suffered from 'the noisomeness' of the prison which was now
made worse by the 'heats of the summer'. For these reasons
he appealed to Charles's 'princely inclination to pity'. His
freedom, he said, was essential 'to the recovery of his health',
and he asked leave 'to abide in such places as he shall be advised

by his physicians'. In conclusion he protested that as he was already in duty bound, he should 'daily most heartily pray for his Majesty's long life and happiness'.

It is unlikely that Morse exaggerated his condition. There can be little doubt he would have died if he had been compelled to endure longer the hardships of Newgate—the vermin, the unwholesome air, the riot of drinking and debauchery. Since his arrest he had been visited regularly by his two friends, Dr. John More and Dr. Thomas Turner. Now they supported his petition with a medical report which they laid before the King. Morse, they said, was 'very infirm in body and inclining to a consumptive condition'; in fact his weakness was so far advanced that their remedies could do nothing for him unless he were given 'the liberty of fresh air and freedom from the closeness and noisomeness of the prison'.

The petition was effective. At eight o'clock in the morning of Saturday, 17 June, Morse, in the custody of the keeper of Newgate, presented himself at Windebank's house in Westminster. There he was formally released, on the understanding that he gave security to appear before the Council within twenty days should he be summoned. Throughout his tenure of office Windebank had showed great friendliness to Catholics. He now acted on verbal instructions from the King. Morse had to wait another four days before the King's formal order for his discharge was delivered to the keeper of Newgate. The pardon, the King stated, was granted 'at the instance of our dearest consort, the Queen', the chief benefactor of Morse's plague-stricken Catholics.

What happened immediately after his release is obscure. For the first twelve months Morse remained in London. He was assured of the King's protection; moreover, he had bound himself to appear when summoned by the Council.

.   .   .   .   .   .

The plague was now over. Life in the city was again normal.

It was not unfitting that as the personal rule of Charles I drew to a close, there occurred the death of Fr. Richard Blount. The old man died on 13 May 1638. He was in his seventy-fifth year: his sickness was hastened by the severity with which he observed the Lenten fast. During Mass on Passion Sunday he had a seizure: his right side became paralysed. But his constitution was strong and he fought off death until Pentecost. By the Queen's permission, perhaps by her command, the funeral was celebrated in the royal chapel, and 'late one evening with the full ceremonial of Catholic burial Fr. Blount was laid to rest; the voices of his brethren mingled with those of the Capuchin friars in that commendation of a departed soul that for so long a time had been uttered only in secret and almost in whispers'. With all the priests of the London district, Morse attended. After the service Fr. Blount's body was buried in one of the cemeteries attached to the Queen's chapel: there, normally, only the Catholic officers and servants of her Court were interred. But Blount had served the Queen and her husband well, and the privilege was extended to him.

In 1639 Morse's name appears in a list of Jesuits working in the south-west of England. He may have been sent there to benefit from 'the fresh air and freedom' which his doctors had recommended. It was the district in which his brother William worked, and comprised Devon and Cornwall, with its headquarters at Exeter, where Francis Wallis, who had been Rector at Liège when Fr. Morse was Minister there, resided as Superior. As in East Anglia, the mission in the south-west was pivoted on a few Catholic families. In Devon there were centres at Ugbrooke, the residence of Lord Clifford of Chudleigh, at Calverleigh, near Tiverton, and at Arlington, the two seats of the Chichester family, and at Teignmouth. In Cornwall, stations can be traced at Fowey, Trevethick, Tor Abbey and Lanherne, where the name of Arundel was sufficient protection for the quiet practice of religion in a large area. As early as March 1628 John Chichester of Arlington and his wife Anne had purchased from Charles I a licence to 'commit Popery' for a yearly sum payable to the Crown. But now that the quarrel between Charles and his Parliament was drawing near, such licences gave little protection. It was known that men like John Chichester were preparing for war. When, after Morse's return to London, the first alarm was raised in the West Country, Arlington was raided. There, and at Mr. Courtenay's, a recusant neighbour at West Molland House, 'more substantial armour' was found 'than in the whole county, the gentry excepted'.

In the spring or early summer of 1640 Morse was back in London, recovered in health. The city was excited. The Scottish army, determined to throw off episcopacy and the service book, had crossed the Tweed at Coldstream. Orders had been issued for the raising of three thousand men from the trained bands. Boys from Christ's Hospital were being taught to play the fife and drum, weapons were marked, musters held in Goodman's Fields and elsewhere. On 17 June Morse was again arrested.

Newton, frustrated by the King, had now sought the support of the Archbishop. Morse recounts the incident. 'I was arrested', he says, 'on a mandate of the High Commission by a man called Longeville.' Thus Morse refers to Fr. Thomas Longeville, his fellow-student in Rome, whose insulting words to Fr. Fitzherbert had precipitated the troubles at the English College. Now, as Morse explains, he was 'assistant to Thresher, the pursuivant in the service of Sir John Lambe, her Majesty's Chancellor.' It is not known when they had last met; but it was Gray, Newton's companion, now dismissed and disgraced, who recognised him. 'Both Longeville and Gray were shameless in their speech,' writes Morse, 'and in the way they set about me. Thresher, on the other hand, was more urbane. They offered to accept twenty shillings and let me go free. But I was also to give assurances to appear in court when summoned. They had no authority to act thus, although in fact they had done so in other cases.'

Morse declined to buy himself off. Arrested with him was another priest, Fr. John Goodman, a cousin of Godfrey Goodman, Bishop of Gloucester. Like Morse, he had on a previous occasion been arrested by John Gray.

'On the eighteenth', Morse continues, 'they brought me before the Archbishop of Canterbury and other members of the Court of High Commission, where I pleaded the freedom granted me under the King's own hand and the security of a thousand pounds that had been given in my name. And because I had committed no offence against the King I expected the Lord Archbishop of Canterbury and his court to grant me the favour which the King himself had been graciously pleased to bestow. Canterbury, however, answered that he had no intention of being compelled to act thus. At this I protested that I had been released by his Majesty, whose protection I now enjoyed. But his Lordship of Canterbury retorted that that was a point for the cognisance of another court, but one that carried no weight in his. And with this he ordered me to be taken back to Newgate.'

There was little else that Laud could do. The city was in a ferment against him. The release of Morse at this moment would place him at the mercy of the mob. Only five weeks earlier a group of agitators, infuriated by the imprisonment of the four aldermen who had resisted the compulsory loan of £100,000 for the Scottish war, had called on all 'lovers of liberty' to assemble in St. George's Fields, Southwark, early on 11 May. Their violence had been restrained by trained bands during the day; but at night, when the soldiery retired, the mob had marched to Lambeth. Warned in time, Laud had fled across the river to Whitehall. There was still danger that his palace would be burned down.

Such was the background of the first meeting between Morse and Laud. 'The next day', Morse continues, 'a rescript called a *Mittimus* was sent to the keeper of my prison. Its tenor was this: I had been arrested, brought before the Court of High Commission and charged with being a priest. I had confessed to the fact, and on that account had been sent to Newgate until it should be determined what was to be done with me. Actually on none of these issues had I been examined; but all that happened was that the King's advocate asked me whether I was a Jesuit. As he put the question while his Lordship of Canterbury was actually speaking, I asked to be allowed to listen to Canterbury, and the question was not put to me a second time.'

Morse was still in Newgate on 1 July. Confined with him was a relation of the pursuivant Thresher. 'This man', explains Morse, 'offered to get me set at liberty again if for this service I agreed to pay him a certain sum of money.' Morse decided 'to negotiate with him'. But on 1 July, after making this entry in his diary, he added a postscript. 'But from the information I now have, this will not be necessary, for Lady Cornwallis . . . has undertaken to see that I am set at liberty, and she has already put my case in the hands of Sir Gregory Fenner, whose good offices the Queen employed on the occasion of my previous imprisonment. This gentleman has no doubt that he will get me released very shortly.'

Fenner, who in 1637 had presided over the commission appointed to inquire into the conduct of Newton's company, was equally concerned to secure the release of Fr. Goodman. 'The same day', continues Morse, 'the keeper of the prison who hitherto had proclaimed that we would be brought to the Assizes that are being held today at Newgate, now denies it; and it is certain this will not happen on account of what occurred yesterday at the sessions in Hicks Hall. For no formal charge was then made—a necessary preliminary to proceedings here—either against us or against any of the forty Catholics who had been delated by [the pursuivant] Pulford. The reason was that many of them had been illegally arrested on the false testimony of perjured witnesses, and they say that the Judges of that court rounded on Pulford as a man unfit to enjoy the authority vested in him by the King. This is all due to the prudent action of the illustrious lord, Baron Herbert, the eldest son of the Earl of Worcester, who is much favoured by the King. For he drew up a petition in which he uncovered the whole of Pulford's iniquitous activity. He then presented it to his Majesty and arranged for it to be shown to five members of the Council, thus laying before them a complete and irrefutable dossier.'

Goodman and Morse were released on 3 July, with the victims of the priest-catcher Pulford, on a warrant from Secretary Windebank.

Six years later at the trial of Laud, Newton brought evidence which formed the seventh charge against the Archbishop. He had then recently secured Morse's indictment and now accused Laud of failing to bring the Jesuit to justice. To support the accusation John Thresher was called in as witness. Convincingly, Laud cleared himself of the charge that he had quashed Thresher's warrant and had been instrumental in the priest's release. Morse, the Archbishop rightly stated, was taken back from Lambeth to Newgate: if he was later discharged, it was the work of Mr. Secretary Windebank and was 'nothing to me'. 'Where my fault was in all this', he wrote, 'I do not yet see . . . I was complained of to the Queen; and a great lady, who perhaps made the complaint, stood by and made herself merry to hear me chid.' This was Lady Cornwallis. Morse, who makes no complaint of Laud's conduct, would have been embarrassed that the treatment he received at the Archbishop's hands should have led to the prelate's discomfiture before the ladies-in-waiting of the Queen.

Early next year Morse crossed once again to the Continent. It was no longer possible for him to work unmolested in London. In November there were rumours of a Popish plot. On the eleventh the Ten-Mile Act, restricting the movements of Catholics, was enforced by proclamation. The growing distrust was heightened by an unfortunate attack made by a member of Parliament who, acting as a Justice of the Peace, had prepared a list of recusants living in the city. Parliament was excited. Sir Isaac Pennington, the city's chief representative in the Commons, offered members, on behalf of the city, a guard of three hundred citizens. At first prepared to accept it, the Commons finally followed saner counsel. But it was the fate of Fr. Goodman, again in Newgate after a brief respite, that finally decided that Morse should go into exile.

In the January sessions at the Old Bailey, Goodman was condemned to be hanged, drawn and quartered as a priest. It was the first sentence that Newton had secured. A few days later Fr. Goodman was reprieved by the King, 'whereupon', wrote a Londoner to his friend in the country, 'the city absolutely refused' to send in the money collected for the war loan. 'The issue of it', the writer predicted, 'will be that in a day or two the man will be hanged or we shall have our money.' The King was faced with a choice between his £60,000 and the priest's life. To save the King, Goodman with uncommon greatness of mind petitioned Charles 'to remit his mercy rather than let him live the subject of so great discontent in your people against your Majesty' and he explained that 'it hath pleased God to give me the grace to desire with the prophet, *That if this storm be raised for my sake, I may be cast into the sea, that others may avoid the tempest.*' The priest's noble gesture split the Lords from the Commons. Charles played for time: he promised a proclamation against the Jesuits and simultaneously offered to submit Goodman's case to the decision of both Houses. Happily for Goodman the City and the Commons soon found a more important scapegoat in Strafford. Goodman was left to languish in peace in prison. But his case and the temper of the city made Morse's presence an embarrassment to the King. The next month, possibly at his own suggestion, he went once again into exile.

15

CHAPLAIN IN THE FIELD

THE same year Morse was again campaigning in Flanders. It was probably at his own request that he was appointed a second time chaplain to the English troops; it was arduous work and he was now in his forty-seventh year.

It was a fruitless warfare endlessly renewed summer after summer. The generalship of Frederick Henry, Prince of Orange, working in alliance with the French could achieve nothing, although in the summer of 1641, when Morse again joined the forces of the Catholic States, the bells rang out in all the Dutch towns and thanksgivings were ordered for the capture of Gennep, the Spaniards' most northerly outpost on the river Meuse. Guelder was next threatened; then Hulst; in the next year Ghent and Bruges. But as soon as the Spanish army appeared, Frederick Henry fell back on the defensive. He had insufficient money to sustain a campaign; moreover he was nearing sixty, he was suffering from gout, and each year he became less capable of the bold strategic measures needed to conclude the war.

Morse was now attached as chaplain to Henry Gage's English regiment. Two years younger than Morse, Gage's principal interests were fighting and religion. From the Jesuit school at St. Omer, he had gone to Italy to study the art of war under Piccolomini, the uncle of the great Duke of Amalfi.

At the age of twenty-two he had joined the Spanish garrison holding Antwerp, where his 'gallant carriage' brought him endearments 'very singular and seldom gained by strangers from the Spanish nation'. At the banquet that followed the relief of the city the Spanish Governor paid tribute to his skill and 'gloried to have been tutor to so brave a soldier'. Thereafter he remained in Spanish service until 1630, when Sir Edward Parham raised an English regiment by licence of Charles I. His serjeant-major was Thomas Tresham, and Gage his commandant. On Parham's death, Tresham took over the regiment and Gage succeeded to Tresham's post. The two worked in harmony and gave decisive help to the Spanish forces when Maastricht was besieged by the States army. Impressed by Gage's performance, the Spanish Commander, the Marquess de Santa Cruz, had persuaded him to raise his own regiment in England. Charles I consented. Recruitment was slow, and by the time of Tresham's death he had enlisted only nine hundred men. Then the remainder of Tresham's troop was amalgamated with his own recruits to form a single English regiment.

It was this force that Morse joined as chaplain in 1641. The relations between the two men were those of mutual esteem. Gage referred to his chaplain as 'the holy Father'; Morse admired the Colonel's reverence for Charles I, since he 'could not be won to do anything against his natural sovereign or inconsistent with the interest and honour of his nation'. For instance, in 1625, on the declaration of war with Spain, he had returned immediately to England and had 'readily left his whole fortune behind him, yea, his wife and children as well as his command'. More recently, when the English regiment had been ordered into Germany, he 'stoutly refused . . . alleging it to be unreasonable for English subjects to maintain a war in the Palatinate against the nephews of his own sovereign'.

Morse, who prepared Gage's men by confession for the battle-
field, appreciated also the officer's complementary concern for
their temporal comfort. Since the Spanish government was
never prompt in the payment of its mercenaries, Gage during
the winter months 'was at Court perpetually, soliciting on
behalf of his soldiers, for their pay, accommodations in garri-
sons, for recruits and the like'. At other times, in the intervals
of campaigning, Gage would stay in his tent, constantly
'studying the classics of military strategy to make himself
master of the theory of war'.

In another tent Morse heard confessions and celebrated
Mass. But even on foreign soil spies mingled with his military
congregation. Both he and his fellow-chaplain, Fr. Peter
Wright, were dogged by a discontented Dominican, Thomas
Gage, the brother of their Colonel. Ten years later, when
Peter Wright stood his trial at the Old Bailey, Friar Thomas
Gage, who had now apostatised and joined the company of
Newton and Mayo, came forward as the principal witness for
the prosecution. With Morse and Wright he had been with
the Spanish army outside Salle. He described how a chapel
was set in a tent, where several times he watched Fr. Wright
say Mass and knew that he heard confessions. As there was no
denying it, Wright at his trial confessed to the charge, courageously using the occasion to pay tribute to his commander,
his accuser's brother, a man 'that for his civil and noble
carriage was esteemed not only by the party for which he
fought, but also by his enemies.'

After their encounter outside Salle, Peter Wright invited
Thomas Gage to the house of the English Jesuits at Ghent. It
was to this community that Morse, Latham, Wright and the
other priests serving the soldiers belonged. Here, during the
winter season, the camp missioners assembled the soldiers and
gave them in groups of ten to twenty the *Spiritual Exercises*

of St Ignatius. In this work they were assisted by the Tertians —the young Fathers who, on completing their studies at Liège, were now for the space of ten months preparing themselves by a second noviceship for the English mission. Here also converts were instructed—in one year, 1640, according to the records of the house, the Tertians and chaplains, working among the Irish, Scotch and Spanish troops, 'received no less than one hundred Protestant soldiers into the Church'. It was the house where Morse rested in the intervals of his winter journeys to the scattered and improvised hospitals. During the winter of 1642 the writer of the house journal notes: 'The labour of the Fathers was principally devoted to the English soldiers in hospitals, though much good was done among the country population. About one hundred Protestants were admitted into the Church. The camp mission produced great fruit, fifty-nine soldiers becoming Catholics.'

It is a bare statement of a chronicler; unrecorded were the toil, the nights by the bedside of the dying troopers, the unending journeys from billet to billet in a bare disfigured countryside.

Three summers in succession Henry Gage's regiment had been employed to succour Guelder, which was invested by the States' army. This was before Morse became his chaplain. Guelder was now fallen, the battle of Rocroi lost. Gage, with his own regiment and fourteen hundred other horse, was despatched to secure Guelderland. It was thought that the Dutch would follow up their victory by occupying the province, but as the author of Gage's brief biography explains, getting wind of Gage's operations, 'they waived their design and returned back with their army into Flanders'. The Colonel then made a quick detour, and joined with Don Francisco de Melo's army 'before the enemy was able to effect anything'.

In the year 1641 he marched to the Dutch border with a

mixed English and Spanish force. He gave alarms everywhere then returned home to winter. An incident in this retreat, recorded by his biographer, was witnessed by Morse. Detailed to 'reduce a castle', Gage did so. Although he forced the defenders to surrender upon discretion, 'he used them with so much generosity that during their captivity he entertained the officers every day at his own table'. For them and the common soldiers, above a hundred in number, he obtained a 'daily allowance'—a courtesy which moved Frederick Henry, Prince of Orange, 'to use principal Spanish officers taken at the latter end of that year's field with like courtesy'.

It was perhaps the most remarkable measure of humanity in the Netherlands war. Hitherto there had been scanty discrimination between man, woman and child. During the few remaining years of his life Morse would have remembered vividly the scenes of slaughter and riot, and perhaps, like Fr. Peter Wright, have drawn on these recollections to illustrate his sermons to his small English congregations. The scenes at the sack of Tuelmont, a small village in Brabant, haunted Wright for many years afterwards, but they were not untypical: 'What cruelty soever hath been committed by any tyrant, what rape, what beastliness by any savage or brutish man, what sacrilege soever by Jew, Turk or infidel were there also committed' by the Dutch, the 'followers of these new Gospellers'. And without sparing the sensitivity of his hearers, he continued his description. 'To lock up hospitals and burn both lame, maimed and sick alive was nothing; to pluck young infants from their mothers' breasts and by their legs fling them up in the air and catch them on their dagger's point was common; to kill young and old, little and great, of all sexes was their sport.' It was not so much rape that horrified the chaplain, but the place and manner of the assault, for the soldiers 'had no horror or scruple to ravish chaste matrons and

violate virgins publicly in the churches and chapels, and after
they had by multiplicity of those obscene acts killed them,
afterwards brutishly to abuse their bodies'. And—it made him
'tremble' to recall it—'they dreaded not in the most vile manner which could be invented to abuse Christ Our Lord in the
Blessed Sacrament', and all this was done 'not by the private
soldier alone or upon the sudden, or in the height of fury, but
in cold blood, after three days' consult, by approbation of all
their officers'. It was all the more remarkable then that Henry
Gage, in co-operation with his chaplains, did something to
make victors more humane.

The operations of each succeeding year enhanced Gage's
reputation as a soldier. As soon as Charles I raised his standard
at Nottingham, Gage did all he could 'to further and advance
the quarrel of his sovereign' in what he called 'this horrible
and unnatural rebellion'. From the Dutch Republic the Parliamentary forces drew a large supply of arms; thus by raids
and other operations carried out independently of the Spanish
commander, Gage was able 'at sundry times to deprive the
rebels of nearly 30,000 arms and to afford his Majesty eight
thousand of those that were intended to be borne against
him'. Inevitably the King summoned him to return, for these
last actions overcame the lingering prejudices of the Royalists
who considered it unwise to entrust a Catholic soldier with a
responsible command. As his biographer states, his recent
conduct in the Netherlands was 'an eternal argument of his
loyalty and prudence'.

The English regiment was now weakened. The civil war
made recruitment impossible. Whenever any member of the
regiment gave his commander 'any probable hopes of attain-
ing his Majesty's army . . . he cheerfully gave him his pass and
encouragement to depart'. With more than two hundred
officers either on their way to England or already fighting in

the King's army, he could no longer maintain a composite force in the field. Taking the best of his men that remained, Gage crossed to England. Peter Wright followed him and continued to serve as chaplain in and about Oxford, where Gage had been given command.

In the interval of waiting for orders to return to England, Morse visited and gave retreats to the English nuns at Ghent and Antwerp. At Ghent were two daughters of Mrs. Dorothy Lawson, his former hostess at St. Anthony's. They belonged to a young and flourishing community of Benedictine nuns, affiliated to its parent English house at Brussels and soon to become in turn the parent of other convents at Boulogne, Dunkerque and Ypres. Here, through the grill in the convent parlour, Morse listened to the sisters he had known and taught as children describe the funeral of their revered mother. She had died on Palm Sunday 1632. It was a saintly death and was said to have been followed by miracles. Her obsequies recalled the pomp of Catholic days. Her body had been carried to Newcastle in her own boat, accompanied by more than twenty barges bearing the mourners. Along the river banks, on either shore, a troop of horsemen had been posted; and, on arriving after nightfall at Newcastle, the family 'found the streets shining with tapers, as light as if it had been noon. The magistrates and aldermen, with the whole glory of the town, which was second only to London, attended at the landing-place to wait on the coffin and there received it covered with a fine black velvet cloth and a white satin cross and carried it but to the church door . . . where they delivered it to the Catholics, who with a priest laid it with Catholic ceremonies to the grave.' It was an uncommon act of homage by the same aldermen who, only six years earlier, had sentenced her chaplain to imprisonment in the city gaol.

These recollections increased Morse's restlessness to return to England. Though his spiritual work was appreciated by the Benedictines at Ghent and by the English Carmelites at Antwerp—he acted for a few weeks as their chaplain and formed with them spiritual bonds which sustained him in the last months of his life—he was aware that his work lay among his people in his own country. Gage was with the King now, and his force disbanded. Morse pleaded again to be allowed to return. It could no longer be urged that his presence in England would embarrass Charles's relations with his Parliament.

Moreover Morse had something of the mystic's sense of destiny. Already he had been exiled three times and had once stood trial for his life; now during his weeks of waiting at Ghent he seems to have had some premonition of martyrdom. It was not that he proposed to court death, but simply that he knew before the event that, despite his efforts to evade arrest, arrested he would be and hanged solely for his priesthood. Tyburn was far removed from the Teresian convent at Antwerp—there was no certainty then that he would ever return to England—but in prayer in the chapel and corridors of the Jesuit house at Ghent and in the cloisters of the English ladies, he realised the end that awaited him and rejoiced. 'Nothing more was in his prayers', writes his biographer, 'than this, that he should be allowed to return to the assistance of his own country. And when he begged frequently and with great earnestness this favour from his Superiors, at last it was decided to give him his holy wish. In the year 1643 he was told at Ghent to prepare himself to return to England. He leapt with joy of soul, then fell to his knees and gave long thanks to God. He spoke about the "most wonderful news". He could not restrain himself. He went round all the Fathers' rooms and all the servants' rooms and told them the happy news. He had a reasonable, nay, almost certain hope that he was returning to martyrdom.'

In this last phrase his biographer reveals what theologians sometimes term a vocation to martyrdom. The simplicity of character which this account reveals is perhaps an essential trait of all martyrs, so frequently do they look forward to their death with enduring desire. To Morse and to all of them the supreme witness they were called to give to their faith in Christ was the only satisfying end to their saintly apostolate. During his last eighteen months, in Cumberland, Newcastle and London, his life follows a pattern which is none of his making, but nevertheless is foreseen and desired.

'The sufferings of the Fathers in England,' writes the chronicler of the Jesuit house at Ghent, 'and the sanguinary death by which some of them had recently crowned their missionary career served only to increase the ardour of the Jesuit Fathers for the English mission. Many Catholic exiles from England joined the community in the prayers offered in the Church for the sufferers in England. Three of the Tertians joyfully received leave to go to England. They were accompanied by Fr. Henry Morse.'

16

LAST ARREST

THE biographers of Morse do not reveal how he and the other three Fathers from Ghent crossed to England. But it is almost certain that they obtained a passage in one of the vessels escorting the Queen out of Holland where for twelve months she had been collecting arms in her husband's cause. It is known that the Fathers left the Continent and arrived in the north of England at the same time as the Queen, and that no other shipping was available at the time. There were Capuchins from the Queen's chapel on board her flagship; they were acquainted with Morse, and it is likely that by their means a passage was arranged.

The Queen sailed from Scheveningen, two miles distant from The Hague, on 19 January 1643. Her fleet comprised nine men-of-war and five transports with horses, baggage and munitions. The wind was slack and little way was made the first day. The next morning a storm arose and 'continued very vehement and terrible', so that for five days together the ships 'were tossed and driven to and fro on the Dogger Sands, not able to make any sail with safety' for fear of being 'underset by sudden gusts and blasts'. With great skill Admiral Martin Tromp, 'careful of his royal charge', brought back his fleet safely into home waters, except for two transports, carrying horses and their grooms, that had been driven aground on the Dutch coast. 'All they in Holland,' wrote a witness of the incident, 'not having ever known a greater storm, were very jocund and joyful to see' the Queen in safety.

On 16 February she again embarked, watched by two Parliamentary ships, the *Providence* and the *Greyhound*, lying a few miles offshore. But 'with a most blessed weather, on a quiet sea, by a soft and gentle gale' the fleet made good way and 'was brought within sight of Flamborough Head'. The Queen had planned to disembark at Newcastle, but as the wind was now blowing from the north she decided instead to continue her journey overland. Accordingly she anchored at Bridlington and was welcomed by the news that the Marquess of Newcastle, following his victory at Stamford Bridge, had made his way into the West Riding. Two days later she drove out from Bridlington in a coach to meet the army 'which welcomed her into the field with many hearty acclamations and expressions of joy'. After riding 'through and through its ranks, even to the new raised and unarmed companies', she returned that night to her quarters on the quay.

'But she had another manner of salutation sent her from the sea the next morning.' For, alerted by the *Providence*, 'four ships and a pinnace, voluntaries in the Parliamentary service, which came overnight into the road, betwixt five and six of the clock next morning, made above an hundred shots at the houses on the quay, for two hours shooting cross bar-shots and many bullets of twelve pounds weight and thereabouts all the while'. Hurriedly leaving her quarters, the Queen sought shelter behind the brow of a hill until the bombardment was over.

The Sunday following her return she again impressed the people of Bridlington by allowing service to be held at her Court, for the parish Church was considered unsafe. At this 'the country people wondered much, who believed all with the Queen to be Papists'.

.   .   .   .   .

Since Morse was too familiar a figure in London to work there in security, he was assigned instead to the northern district. Durham and Northumberland, and parts perhaps of Cumberland and Westmorland—the four counties that comprised the 'College of St. John the Evangelist'—were already known to him from his days at St. Anthony's; so also were many of the missionaries. Richard Holtby was now dead; it was his successor, Fr. Christopher Simpson, who welcomed Morse early in 1643 and posted him to the Cumberland area.

Simpson did not possess the legendary prowess of Holtby, but by his evident uprightness he had won for himself a position of great esteem in the border counties, so much so that he was said to have 'drawn to himself many of the leading men among the heretics'. Later, after he had established a clandestine academy for the education of young Catholic boys, many non-Catholics also 'did not hesitate to entrust their sons to his teaching'. He was nine years younger than Morse, a former student of St. Omer's and of the English College, Rome, where he had begun his studies for the priesthood in the year of Morse's ordination.

At the time of Morse's return there were ten Jesuits serving the four counties. Five more were added in the following year, and together they formed one of the most remarkable communities of missionary priests to be found anywhere in England. There was Fr. Thomas Rochester, an adopted son of Roger Widdrington, a man of humble origin who (it was said) 'toiled with indefatigable industry amid the midnight snows and northern cold for full forty years'. In the western part of the district, he was all that Fr. Ralph Corby, a man of Morse's age, was to the people of Durham—'in paradise among the poor people'. With Fr. Rochester worked Fr. Thomas Gascoigne, a Yorkshireman, known as the apostle of the poor, and others who had received their first training from Fr. Holtby.

Even before the outbreak of war this district was considered the poorest in England. 'They have no constant or regular alms,' the Provincial reported; 'they depend manifestly on divine providence, which suffers them not to do without at least sufficient food and clothing to keep them alive.' From 1643 the conditions became markedly worse. Scottish raiders now crossed the border more frequently 'to the great terror of the inhabitants generally, and especially the Catholics. Against them they swore utter extermination. They broke into their houses, tore up the very floors, and searched every part so closely that they discovered books, vestments and other things that had been concealed from the English pursuivants.' The author of the yearly report wrote in understatement when he complained that 'these violent proceedings greatly increased the dangers of the Fathers'. Their ministry, in fact, was almost at a standstill. 'Many Catholics feared to admit them to their houses to offer the Holy Sacrifice or even to administer the sacraments to them.' Yet this outbreak of more violent persecution, which coincided with Morse's return to the north, brought the customary compensations to the priests. 'Protestants who before had been hesitating', it was said, 'were brought to the determination to enter the Catholic Church, and many Catholics who had neglected their duty were aroused to reform their lives.'

Further distress was brought on the northern counties by the loss of all trade with the south. As long as Newcastle remained in the hands of the King no colliers could sail to London. In 1641 more than three thousand ships had entered the Tyne, most of them coastal vessels; but in the twelve months preceding Morse's arrival there were hardly three or four ships to be seen a week. Moreover, the withdrawal of the Scots army at the same time brought further confusion to the city. Already the market for coals had collapsed; a bushel, selling for sixpence, meant ruin to the coal-owners and miners alike. Now alehouse-keepers, who had prospered while there were troops in the town, were distracted for lack of custom. 'They see their ale turn sour for want of good fellows', wrote the reporter in *Exceeding True Newes from Newcastle*. 'Their beer is converted into vinegar.' Finally, in the same year, there was a fresh outbreak of plague in Durham and Newcastle.

It was perhaps this last event that determined Fr. Christopher Simpson to post Morse to the eastern part of the district, for his recovery from the plague was too recent to justify the risk of placing him in an infected town.

But there was poverty and misery enough in the country areas to satisfy his passion for the poor. There are few records of Cumberland houses, such as St. Anthony's in Northumberland, which were secure bases for a rural apostolate. All that his biographers say is that for a year and a half, or longer, Morse gave a 'remarkable example to his brethren, doing all that was asked of a most faithful and hard-working priest'. Probably, like Fr. Gascoigne, he lived simply in some cottage or small room placed at his disposal by local Catholics. The experiences of the two priests were similar, except that Gascoigne endured the hardships of the mission for nearly forty years, 'every month making excursions extending some two hundred miles, over mountains and by precipices, through snow, floodwater and rough tracks almost impassable in winter time. On these dangerous journeys he often had to accept the poorest of accommodation for the night.' At home, in his room that 'resembled more a cave', he had to cover his roof with bark and hew wood for his fire, to find some protection against the cold.

At this time and for a century afterwards Cumberland, to the south of Carlisle as far as Penrith, was 'mostly an open country, full of commons', and to the north, an almost impenetrable morass, which was crossed only by paths known to mosstroopers, smugglers, pedlars and priests. Here cavalry of the Scottish raiders roamed freely. Although at first the battle was far away from Carlisle, in the second year of the war the country around the city, which was Morse's district, saw several engagements. Sir Wilfrid Lawson attempted to seize the city for Parliament, advancing along the Roman Wall, still largely intact, and still, as Sir William Brereton declared, 'the strongest fortification I have ever met in England'. But his force was defeated and driven back from the city to Abbey-holme. In the next year the whole country between Newcastle and Carlisle was distraught. The gentry were under arms, with their neighbours and tenants. Newcastle was besieged: if New-castle fell, Carlisle would fall also. It was at this time that Morse was captured. He was answering the call of a sick Catholic who lived on the borders of Durham and Cumber-land, when he walked into a party of soldiers detached from the Parliamentary forces marching against Carlisle. It was late in the evening, and it was immediately suspected that he was a priest, for it was considered improbable that anyone but a priest would be about after dark unescorted and unarmed. Moreover there was a rumour in the neighbourhood that a priest would be visiting this very house, and accordingly a guard had been mounted at the entrance. As usual Morse refused to reveal his priestly character. The soldiers, therefore, ordered him to Durham for examination; but as it was too dark to make the journey that night, they decided to lodge at the house of the local justice of the peace. The place is not named, nor the official, who was away from home. His wife, however, was there—a Catholic lady, who received Morse with great kindness. She guessed that he was a priest, but no question was asked. By her mere attention to him she indicated privately what she thought: the best bedroom in the house was offered him, a bright fire lit, and a 'lavish supper' laid out. Then one by one, on trumped-up errands, she sent her servants from the room, then her own children. Left with Morse alone, she stated plainly that she was a Catholic. Then she begged him to say just as plainly whether or not he was a priest: if he was, she would help him to escape before her husband returned. Morse was in a dilemma. Was it a trap of the soldiers to make him confess his priesthood? He refused to reveal himself. The woman persisted. Morse again refused. Finally he took a chance and the lady immediately prepared to make good her promise.

But there was a further problem. Morse was anxious to escape, but he feared that if he did, then his hostess would suffer. He declined her offer. 'But the lady would not hear of this. With courage remarkable in one of her sex', the biographer continues, 'she said that risk did not matter at all. It was uncertain whether she would suffer; but it was certain that she would rather lose everything, fortune, life and all, than hand over an innocent man, and a priest at that, to his enemies.' She took the decision out of Morse's hands by putting immediately in train her plan of flight.

Hidden in the same town were some other Catholics, captured during the previous two days. Already, with the lady's help, they had made good the first stage of their escape. A secret assembly-point outside the town had already been arranged for that night. Thither the lady conducted Morse, 'taking little-known tracks'. When all the party was gathered, Morse took a hurried farewell of his hostess of a few hours, and prayed God to reward her abundantly for her courage. She then returned to await her husband. That night Morse and his party put fourteen miles between the town and their shelter for the following day.

For the next six weeks the hunt persisted. Although the

Scots had been in the district since January, it was only in June that serious preparations were made for the reduction of Newcastle. It was essential that the town should be reduced quickly if London was to have coal the following winter. Morpeth, seized early in the year by Montrose, was recaptured by the Earl of Calendar with his Scottish force on 29 May. Since March the Scots had held South Shields; Montrose's subsequent assault had been repelled and he had been forced to retire before Fairfax into Newcastle. At the beginning of June Calendar crossed the Tyne at Newburn and secured Sunderland. On 2 July the main Royalist army in the north was decisively defeated at Marston Moor, seven miles west of York, by the parliamentary force advancing to join up with the Scottish army. On 24 July Hartlepool and Stockton surrendered. Newcastle was now isolated.

The attack began on the twenty-seventh. That night Calendar entered Gateshead. He had come suddenly up Windmill Hill, surprised the opposing troops, chased them down the other side of the hill, hustled them over the bridge and closed them inside the town. Five batteries were placed on Windmill Hill and others to the east of the bridge, commanding the south walls of the town from Closegate to Sandgate. The next day the bombardment began: 'the cannon did continually extreme good service, not only against the walls and batteries, but also against particular places and persons, besides the frequent shooting of pot-pieces and other fireworks of great importance, which daily annoyed the inhabitants of the town.'

Fenced in on the south by Calendar's troops, its river sealed by ten blockships, Newcastle entered on the last stage of its siege. It was likely to be long for the Tyne divided the Parliamentary troops, who held no bridge. But by an unexpected manœuvre the Scots recrossed the river at Newham on 14 August and took Elswick the following day. Batteries were then placed on high ground to the west between Ousebourn and Pandon; the positions on either bank of the river were connected, and the poor inhabitants who had fled from the lower to the upper town for shelter were bombarded.

Outside Newcastle's massive walls, built without and within of squared stone and strengthened with dungeon towers, the Scottish soldiers were 'accommodated in huts composed of turf, clay, straw and wattles', while officers were lodged in 'circulating pavilions'; other troops were scattered in the villages to the east to watch for any attempt at relief coming from Carlisle, which still held out for the King.

At six points where mines had been sprung the fire of the batteries was concentrated on 19 October. From six in the morning until three in the afternoon the fire was continuous. Finally breeches were made, and after 'a hard dispute' lasting two hours the city was taken, though fighting continued on the walls. At five in the evening plundering began. Sir Thomas Ridell who eighteen years earlier had sat on the Bench of aldermen that had examined Henry Morse, signed the articles of surrender. All Northumberland and Durham was now lost to the King.

For six weeks, while the Scots and Parliamentary troops were in possession of the country to the west of Newcastle, Morse remained in hiding 'in an out-of-the-way corner of his district'. Then, after the fall of the town, 'he determined to move to some other secret place'. As he was unfamiliar with the country he placed himself in the hands of a guide, 'a most trustworthy person'. But a strange providence controlled his movements. Through some stroke of chance or divine interposition (his biographers are at a loss for an explanation) the guide suffered a sudden black-out of memory. Walking ahead of the priest, the man came within a mile or two of the house where he was to conceal his charge, when suddenly he lost all recollection of the road. 'Although he had done the journey many times, he had no idea in which direction the house lay, or which path to take.' Morse, too, was helpless. 'He was being taken to another part of the country where, because he was unknown, he would be able to continue his work as a priest.' There was a cottage in sight. There the guide led Morse to inquire the way. At the door a man confronted them. Scrutinising Morse closely, he asked whether or not he was the man who six weeks before had escaped from the guard that was escorting him to Durham. Morse was unprepared. He could deflect skilfully the direct questions of his judges under examination in court, but, taken unawares in a lonely cottage, he blurted out the truth. 'Yes,' he said.

Morse was taken at once to Durham. 'For several weeks he was lodged in a foul and horrid cell.' It was autumn. Morse suffered from the cold, but his stay in the city was brief. A strange phenomenon occurred during his imprisonment, and it was reported in *The Scottish Dove*. About ten o'clock on the morning of Tuesday, 19 November, 'there appeared three suns, almost a triangle, and a rainbow, with the bend towards the earth, compassing one of the suns within the bow, and the other two ends of the bow going upwards butted one to the end of one sun, and the other to the other.' It was the King's birthday. While varying interpretations were being given to the portent, Morse was transferred to Newcastle.

It was his second experience of Newcastle gaol. During the siege it had been a strong-point and from its walls the King's artillery had pounded the encampment beyond. Although the castle was largely destroyed, the prison at Newgate was still sufficiently secure. St. Andrew's Church was partly in ruins, though there was lesser damage to All Saints where Mrs. Lawson lay buried.

On 19 November Morse and twenty-five others, merchant

princes of Newcastle 'associated with the Royalist cause', were ordered to London in custody. With all Durham and Northumberland in the hands of Parliament, the regular shipment of coals was resumed. In November no ships had left Newcastle for London. In December one hundred and forty-five sailed from the city.

It was in a hastily loaded convoy of colliers that Morse was despatched to London. As he passed down the Tyne he saw on the north bank the recent ruins of St. Anthony's, his first home as a missionary priest. The Scottish soldiers had razed it to the ground. Then on past the point where Dudley Swan had boarded the *Sea Horse*, and past Tynemouth Castle, so recently dismantled, and the priory, only ten years before 'one of the finest churches in the country' but now in ruins. Off the Yorkshire coast the convoy ran into a gale; one ship foundered, but the collier in which Morse was a passenger was able to make Yarmouth for refitting.

17

NEWGATE

At Yarmouth lived George Morse, the fourth of Henry's nine brothers. He was now one of the principal men in the town and played a considerable part in its administration. He was unmarried, and his great wealth, drawn from herring fleets, was later bequeathed to his nephews, the sons of his three married sisters.[1]

Immediately on the arrival of the collier, George Morse sent to Norwich to inform their eldest brother Robert. Like George he was a Protestant, though he held Henry in great affection. On boarding the ship they learned from their brother of 'the barbarous usage' he had suffered from the crew. Robert 'did everything he could to secure the priest's release, for he was an eminent lawyer. He provided him with all he immediately needed, and for his future wants gave him ample money, which Henry later gave away to the poor.' As there was little more he could do in Yarmouth, he distributed money to the sailors on an understanding that for the rest of the voyage they should treat his brother with greater humanity; he then left for London by road.

The collier sailed on. The crew persisted in their brutal treatment. In London they handed over their prisoner to the

[1] A silver salver, now among the plate of the Corporation, was once in the possession of George Morse.

magistrates. 'We have done our job,' they are reported to have said. 'Now go and do yours. Hang the man if you wish.'

After a night on board Morse was taken to Newgate. On the way he was given permission by his escort to pay his respects to the Count Egmont, Duke of Guelders, the Spanish Ambassador to England since 1640. Morse did not know him personally but received a request from him to call as soon as his ship docked in London. Like several foreign noblemen, Egmont had always manifested a protective interest in priests and, as often as possible, was a devout witness to their execution when they came to Tyburn.[1] Now he welcomed Morse with affection, led him into his private suite, and there, after serving his Mass, knelt to receive his blessing and beg his prayers for all the people and business he had most at heart. Through the Count's influence, Morse was then allowed to visit some friends in London. Their names are not given, but no doubt their number included Fr. Wilson, the former Superior of the London Jesuits, and Dr. Turner, who had worked so closely with Morse during the plague. That evening he was taken to Newgate.

Meanwhile his brother Robert had reached London. It had been his hope that he would be able to greet Henry at the port with the news of his release. But the city was in an anti-papal frenzy, making ready for the execution of the Primate, the Romaniser and traitor to the Protestant heritage. In any other month or year Robert, through influence in the courts, might have succeeded. But it was hardly to be expected that the people who were clamouring for Laud's blood would the same week suffer a priest, particularly a Jesuit, to go free. Moreover

---

[1] 'At the time our business detained us in England,' he wrote in 1650, 'we were by a sovereign grace of Almighty God, an eye-witness of the constancy of divers martyrs; and out of the fifteen who from 1640 to the end of 1645 gained the palm of martyrdom in different places, we saw eleven suffer in London.' Foley, vol. I, p. 564.

at the Archbishop's trial one of the accusations concerned
Morse himself. At the instigation of the informer Newton it
had been laid to his charge that he had 'held correspondence'
with Henry Morse 'who had seduced five hundred persons
and more' in St. Giles and Westminster; and, graver still, that
he had concealed a conspiracy against the King in which these
Jesuits had played a chief part.

Robert Morse, besides, had to contend with Francis Newton.
Even if he could come to terms with the magistrates, he was
certain to be foiled by his brother's sworn enemy. Still, Robert
used all possible means to save his brother's life and offered
three hundred pounds to the Mayor, Sheriffs and Recorder of
London for a respite of three days to allow time to procure his
banishment. He offered also to be bound in a penalty of two
thousand pounds to be forfeited in case he returned. He was
daily in touch with Henry who still feared to take any step
that might alter the end God had determined for him. From
Newgate Henry wrote to Fr. Wilson who was now Provincial, 'I wish to know the mind of your Reverence as to
whether I should allow so much endeavour to be made on my
behalf and such extraordinary pains taken, and a bad example
thus to be given. Should I not rather entrust all things to the
holy Providence of God and to the ordinary course of events?
For my part I desire to be dissolved and to be with Christ. But
if I am necessary to my people', he concluded, quoting St.
Martin, 'I do not refuse to labour.' But events took the
decision from the Provincial's hands. Newton had been busy.
On New Year's day 1645 Morse appeared before the magistrates' court of St. Giles-in-the-Fields. The indictment was
read: 'that Henry Morse, late of the said parish, clerk, born
within the kingdom of England and after the feast of St. John
the Baptist, I Elizabeth, and before the said first of January
[1645] made and ordained sacerdos, *anglice*, seminary priest,

was and remained traitorously and as a false traitor of the Lord King,' and so on. . . . The indictment read, Morse was remanded to Newgate.

The following day the Commons in debate established the principle that it possessed the right to declare any crime it pleased treason. On the fourth the House of Lords, under pressure from the Commons passed the ordinance of attainder. The same day Laud was sentenced and another ordinance was passed abolishing the Book of Common Prayer. Thus, declared the *Mercurius Britannicus*, 'the Dad and Darling were both condemned together, both guilty of high treason, the one against the State, the other against God'. On Friday, the tenth, 'the little firework of Canterbury was extinguished on Tower Hill'.

After Laud's execution Newgate became the last stronghold of traditional worship. Catholics, priests and laity alike, crowded the prison. The King's departure had left the Catholics in the capital unprotected. Newton, Mayo, Gray and the other members of the company were free to pursue their victims without fear of reprisal. Fr. William Henderson, a priest of St. Giles-in-the-Fields, had been committed the day that Morse was indicted. In Newgate he joined other London priests—John Hammond, Walter Coleman, Edmund Canam, Andrew Fryer, Edward Tresham, John Abbot, Peter Wilford, James Brown—some no more than names in the lists of the Colleges abroad where they had been trained. Several had lingered many years already in Newgate; others, like Goodman, once again in chains, died this winter.

In addition, there were prisoners who had rebelled against the new Puritanism—both the extreme reformers and the loyal Anglicans. For the first time the Churches were 'sealed up' on weekdays, and a loyal Protestant lamented now that the Londoners' 'apprehension of Popery . . . carried the people so far to the other extreme that they lost all sense of moderation and decorum'.

Also in Newgate now were political prisoners like Mary Hugget, the wife of a labourer in St. Giles, who had declared Parliament 'round-headed rogues' and had invoked God to consume them with a pox. The keeper's income had never been greater, since the prisoners for religion and politics were herded in large numbers in the same quarters as the common thieves. It was during Morse's brief stay in Newgate that Hugh Parsons, sentenced to *peine forte et dure*, because he had refused to plead when charged with stealing, was led out into the prison yard and pressed to death.

Before Morse was brought a second time before the Bench to hear his sentence, he received news of the death of his friend Colonel Gage. On Tuesday 14 January a letter from Major General Browne, the Parliamentary commander at Abingdon, was read in the Commons. It described how Gage, the Governor of Oxford, in company with Prince Rupert, came up against Abingdon on the Culham side with a thousand horse and eight hundred foot. Although they had gained the bridge before the alarm was raised, they had been unable to break it down. To take them in the rear, General Browne sent a force into the meadows which were heavily under water. After a 'hot dispute' lasting four hours he regained the bridge. Among the dead was Colonel Gage. It was said he was slain by a traitor in his own regiment, but this was never established. In Newgate Morse was comforted for the loss by the knowledge that Peter Wright, his fellow-chaplain in the Flanders campaigns, was present at the action. He gave his Colonel his last absolution and blessing and held him in his arms as he died on the field. The Royalists had retired with 'three cartloads of dead'; there were also other fallen, who were 'thrown into the river or carried away on horseback'.

Later in the same week, on Friday the seventeenth, Morse received judgment. Newton's henchmen were present in court—James Wadsworth and Thomas Mayo. At the bar with him stood Susan Platt. Her husband, John, of St. Giles-with-out-Cripplegate, had been apprehended for blasphemy, declaring that to baptise an infant was of no more effect than to baptise a cat or a dog. Now he was 'too feeble to appear at this session without danger to his life', and in his place came Susan, his wife, who had participated in his blasphemy. Also with them was Richard Bemean, charged with uttering 'irreverent words against the Parliament'. They caused little excitement for interest had now shifted to the stationer, Dobson, waiting with Morse to stand his trial before a special Council of War for printing a popular and scandalous book against the Parliament.

The proceedings were brief. There was no trial. The charge against him was read by the Recorder: that, convicted of his priesthood on 13 April in the thirteenth year of Charles I he was reprieved without judgment; since that time he had retired to foreign parts; now he had returned to England. This was a statement of fact. It remained only to ask the prisoner what reply he had to make, and then pass the sentence which the King had mercifully withheld nearly seven years earlier. It was true, Morse replied, that he had previously been convicted of his priesthood, and he added, making the only point that might have carried weight with the Judge: 'The evidence was trivial and the witnesses worthless.' It was his last thrust at Newton. The Judge answered: 'What then? Are you not a priest or do you think the previous conviction should not stand?' With dignity Morse spoke: 'For my part I will make no decision touching myself. I leave everything in the hands of your Lordship.'

The sentence for treason, which could now be interpreted

according to the meaning Parliament gave it, was then pronounced. He had first heard the phrases as a young student of
Barnard's Inn at the trial of John Almond. 'You must go to
the place from whence you came, there to remain until ye
shall be drawn through the open city of London upon hurdles
to the place of execution, and there be hanged and let down
alive, and your privy parts cut off, and your entrails taken
out and burnt in your sight, then your head to be cut off
and your body divided into four parts, to be disposed of at
his Majesty's pleasure. And may God have mercy on your
soul.'

Susan Platt was acquitted; Morse was led back to Newgate.

The prison, says Ambrose Corby, during the four days
between the passing of the sentence and its execution, became
like a market-fair. Any priest condemned to the gallows drew
a crowd demanding his blessing, but Morse was also the hero
of the recent plague. Each visitor paid his fee into the hands
of the gaoler; there was no danger, as in the case of other
prisoners, of any attempt to escape. Indeed, before the war
was over there occurred the famous incident of the seventeen
convicts who had been sentenced together at the Old Bailey.
On the eve of their execution their wives and friends were
admitted to the prison to hear the customary sermon. Under
their coats the ladies carried rapiers which they secretly passed
to the convicts in the course of the sermon. It was seven in
the evening and mid-winter. 'Taking their opportunity', the
account reads, 'they ran violently at the turnkey and the rest
of the keepers, wounded them, and forced their passage down
the stairs, all of them making an escape away.'

Among Morse's visitors were citizens of every class. Some
came from curiosity, others to seek his prayers, or a keepsake
or some message of comfort for their sick friends. They

seemed unconcerned at the risk they incurred; they took no care
to conceal that they were Catholics. 'Especially the day before
he died', the writer continues, 'it was an amazing sight to
watch the people; they came in their hundreds, from the first
hour of the day to the last at night, to congratulate Christ's
athlete on the victory at hand, and to beg his intercession for
themselves and for their suffering country, when he should
enter into heaven.'

With the crowd mingled many Jesuits, probably his brother,
Fr. William Morse, among them; certainly his friend and
fellow-Jesuit, Fr. Thomas Harvey, the brother of the Prioress
of the English Teresians at Antwerp. From 1636 Harvey had
worked in London, and for nine years, at great personal risk
he had acted as an unofficial chaplain at Newgate, caring for
the common criminals lying under sentence of death. Each
year he received more than sixty prisoners into the Church, and
in the course of his apostolate became a constant and voluntary
inmate of the gaol. He visited Morse during his first imprisonment. Now he came again, bringing with him his brother
and the non-Catholic lady with whom he lodged. 'They
desired to put two questions to the Father. The first, whether
a man might be saved by the merits of Christ without praying
to the saints. The second, whether he [Fr. Morse], now about
to die for his religion, believed that he should be damned dying
outside it.' With precision Morse gave the answer of the
Roman theologians of his day. 'A man might be saved by
Christ's merits,' he said, 'without praying to the saints, but
not without believing in the Church's teaching, namely, that
it is both a right and good thing to pray unto saints.' Then he
turned to the second question, and in his reply revealed his
faith in prayer and hinted perhaps at some closely-guarded
experience with God. It was a theme to which he was to return
on the scaffold. 'He was about to die for his religion,' he said;

indeed, the manner of the sentence left no doubt on the point, 'and he was certain there was no salvation outside the Catholic Church, wherein miracles were wrought daily; wherein the blind did see, the dumb spoke, the dead rose again, devils were cast out; and he died to testify to that truth.' And Fr. Harvey concludes, 'He spoke with great fervour though he had neither eaten nor drunk that day.' 'It is difficult', Fr. Ambrose Corby comments, 'to give an idea of the extent to which these calumnies are embedded in the minds of Protestants: that there is insufficient force in the passion of Jesus Christ alone without the merits of the saints, and that none of us can be found to give his life for his religion, as if the mere profession of that religion was sufficient for salvation.'

Fr. Harvey's influence with the Newgate prisoners had brought on him the attentions of Newton who delated him to the Council. In a severely worded warrant made out for the pursuivant, it was ordered that if Harvey was captured, he was to be flogged publicly at the cart's tail along the whole way from Newgate to Tyburn gallows. Now, in his visit to Morse, when the danger of arrest seemed remote, he fell into Newton's hands. It was the pursuivant's last and meanest act of revenge on Morse.

That night Fr. Harvey, his friends and about twenty visitors were detained. It was Morse's last full day in Newgate. 'The mishap troubled the Father', writes Ambrose Corby, 'as much as it did his visitors, for his sympathy for the suffering of others, particularly when it was for his sake, was very great. He urged them to trust in Providence, and promised them that since he had been prevented by the intrusion of the officers from doing anything for them here, he hoped to be a better intercessor for them with God.'

It was not until the next day, after Morse's execution, that they were released on payment of twenty pounds to the gaoler.

But no persuasion or bribe could secure Fr. Harvey his freedom.[1]

On this last day in prison Morse's foreign visitors were treated with a courtesy that was denied to his London friends. Every ambassador of the greater States either came in person to see him, or, if they were detained or out of London, sent a deputy. It was a gesture of sympathy to the Englishman who professed and shared their religion. On later occasions the same scenes were re-enacted, but no such demonstration had occurred hitherto. During the plague Morse had depended in part on the embassies for his funds, and in his ministration to the sick he had not omitted the subjects of France and Spain. 'Now the Ambassadors of the Catholic kings and princes, without a single exception, came and begged his prayers for their own or their rulers' salvation and well-being. There could have been no greater tribute to the outstanding saintliness of the priest and his devotion to the duties of his state; nor a more manifest declaration of the true cause of his death.' The Spanish Ambassador was unable to come in person, but sent several members of his staff to express his homage. With the courtesy of the court he represented, the Marquis de Sabran, Ambassador of Louis XIV, sent first to inquire what hour would be most convenient for the priest to receive him, and when, at the moment of departure, he was delayed by an important visitor, he again sent a messenger to Newgate. Touched by his

[1] Fr. Harvey was a descendant of Sir Nicholas Harvey, Henry VIII's Ambassador to Charles V, and a cousin of the Marquis of Bristol. He had been born, during the exile of his parents, at Mechlin, and on this account claimed to be a subject of the Spanish Crown. He was eventually released through the intercession of the Spanish Ambassador. His sister, Mother Anne of the Ascension, was the first English lady to enter St. Teresa's reformed Carmelites, and was now Prioress at Antwerp, where Morse had been her chaplain. Before leaving Newgate, Morse gave Fr. Harvey a holy picture (now preserved at the Lanherne Carmel) to send to his sister in gratitude for her prayers.

thoughtfulness, Morse handed his secretary a crucifix of silver, with a request that the Ambassador should accept it as a reminder to keep always at heart the protection of the Catholic faith in England.

All that day it rained. The London lanes were thick with mud. In the manner of pilgrims, a Portuguese nobleman and his wife, without escort and in the guise of simple citizens, walked on foot to the prison. The Ambassador of the Holy Roman Empire was out of London. In his place came his secretary. So impressed was he by the calmness of Morse that he returned the same evening and again the following morning an hour before Morse was due to leave for Tyburn. 'Never in my life', he stated, 'have I seen greater resolution in any man, nor a calmer expression on anyone's face; he was so happy and modest and was so affable and kind to all. When I commended to his prayers the Emperor and the house of Austria, he answered that he had always had them at heart, and hoped that they would soon triumph over the enemies of the Church, become her great glory and advance her cause. He said that the Supreme Pontiff would show favour to the house. They were words I listened to intently, as if they augured blessings to come and were spoken in a spirit of prophecy.'

18

TYBURN

On his last day in Newgate Morse had taken neither food nor drink. That night he did not sleep. Until four o'clock in the morning he waited on his visitors, answered their questions, gave advice when it was asked, and replied with courtesy to the inquiries of non-Catholics. And he did this 'as though he had nothing else to do but concern himself with the business of each individual'.

About four o'clock he began his preparation for Mass. As he had done each day of his life—during the plague, in the military encampments and on the Cumberland moors—he recited first the Litany of Our Lady and then the Litany of the Saints for the conversion of England. Surrounded by his friends, he moved to the altar prepared by Fr. Harvey. Although it was the feast of St. Vincent and St. Anastasius, Spanish martyrs of the fourth century, he chose to offer a votive Mass of the Holy Trinity, in recognition, as it were, of the beginning and the consummation of his existence. To the keeping of the Three Divine Persons he committed his friends, with something of the same emotion experienced by Peter Wright when, a few years later, he too said his last Mass in Newgate, and, after the consecration, was seen to break into tears. Though he could endure the prospect of disembowelling it was the thought that he was so soon to be parted from his friends that made him momentarily lose his soldierly control of himself.

The secretary of the Imperial Ambassador was present. Like many others, he had confessed to Morse, and with them he now received Holy Communion from his hands.

When Mass was over Morse spoke to the people. Then he rested for an hour and recited his breviary. This done, he visited the condemned criminals, speaking a word to each and taking his farewell of them 'with so smiling and gentle a countenance that he amazed them all'. He had now only to await the summons to execution. With Fr. Harvey he went apart, and the two priests prayed silently together. Then they moved again among the people.

At nine o'clock, the customary hour, Mr. Gibbs, the sheriff, came to Newgate to lead the prisoner to execution. With relief Morse fell on his knees, joined his hands in prayer, and thanked God in the hearing of all. 'And this he did in such a tone of voice, and with such expression on his countenance, that all present were greatly moved.'

The charity which, as he told his judges, no authority on earth had power to prevent, was again manifested at the end. In Newgate there was a learned Irish Franciscan, Fr. Christopher, from Ulster. He was an exile as well as a prisoner, and Morse saw in this a double claim to kindness. He had been captured in his own country, carried across the Irish Sea, and left in Newgate to die. Singling him out from all the priests and people present, Morse embraced him. Frequently in later years the Franciscan would speak of this moment. 'There was nothing belonging to this world in his expression: his face was so lit up with joy that if I had been a heathen or a heretic, the experience of sweetness I then had would have won me to the faith he professed. And it was not a brief or fleeting experience; it has abided with me to my old age.' This radiance of his countenance was caught in a remarkable portrait done during Morse's last night in Newgate by Mr. Giffard, a Catholic prisoner. Though he was untrained and inexperienced, he achieved an astonishing likeness and recorded something of the luminous quality of his expression.[1]

Taking Morse by the hand as a gesture of respect, Mr. Gibbs led him through the prison gate into the street where four horses, harnessed to a hurdle, were waiting to drag him to Tyburn. The sheriff took some straw in his hands, laid it on the hurdle, and helped Morse to lie down. Then the ropes were fastened round his waist, and the strange cortège, flanked by fifty mounted guards, began its way through the muddy streets to Tyburn.

Passing along Newgate into Holborn, past Gray's Inn, the horses pulled up outside the parish church of St. Giles, and Morse was offered a drink. There he prayed for the souls of all his friends among the poor whom he had helped to die at peace with God. A few hundred yards from Tyburn, the Marquis de Sabran, riding in his coach decked as for a royal occasion, overtook Morse. Momentarily the sheriff pulled up the horses while the Ambassador stepped out into the muddy road and, bending his knee, begged the priest's blessing.

At Tyburn the hurdle halted beneath the gallows. There for half an hour the sheriff waited the arrival of four other criminals. He ordered the crowd back and made a passage for the Ambassador's coach. Through one of his men he inquired whether the Marquis would prefer any other position: if he wished he could draw still closer, so that he could speak to Morse from his coach. The Ambassador then walked through the dirt to the hurdle, and taking Morse by the hand, begged him to remember in his prayers the common peace of the

[1] This portrait hangs in the Convent at Lanherne, Cornwall, where the Antwerp community of Carmelites is now established.

Christian world, his own country of France and his king and queen. Morse consented. He then handed the Ambassador his handkerchief as an earnest of his promise, for it was all he had to give him.

Don Antonio de Sousa, the Portuguese Resident, kept to his coach. He had been commissioned to propose his master's daughter, Catherine, for marriage to Prince Charles, and he now asked Morse to further the project with his prayers.

As Morse rose to his feet he saw the coach of Count Egmont, in whose house he had offered Mass. 'Most illustrious Sir,' he said, speaking in Latin to ensure privacy, 'I shall remember my promise, and when I come before God I shall not be un-mindful of the kindness your Lordship has shown me.' Answering in Latin, the Count congratulated him that he had been allowed to glorify God by a martyr's death. Then after a few further words he took his farewell.

Morse was helped up the ladder on to the cart placed below the gallows. The rope was fastened round his neck. Then he asked the sheriff whether he could address the people. Mr. Gibbs gave leave but on condition that no word was spoken against the King or Parliament or against the laws and government of the country.

While the rope was being fixed on his companions, Morse began: 'I am come hither to die for my religion.' His exact words are not recorded by his biographers. 'For that religion which was founded by Christ, established by the Apostles, and propagated through all the ages since to the present day by a visible hierarchy; a religion that rests on the testimony of the Scriptures, supported by the authority of the Fathers and Councils, outside which there is no salvation.'

The crowd murmured. His words were lost. The sheriff interrupted: 'Mr. Morse, I beg you say nothing that will offend the people. Rather, if you know any treason against the King or Parliament, now that you are on the point of death, declare it.'

'I have a secret to declare which highly concerns his Majesty and Parliament to know', Morse called out. The crowd pressed forward. There was silence.

'Gentlemen, take notice,' Morse continued, 'the kingdom of England will never be truly blessed until it returns to the Catholic and apostolic faith, and until its subjects are all united in one belief and live in obedience to one head, the Bishop of Rome. This is the secret, Sir, if you will have it; this is the treason I have to disclose. Other treason I know none. But I do know for a certainty that the true cause of all the troubles and miseries which the nation groans under at this present time, is heresy—heresy which has grown like a canker through his Majesty's dominions; and till it be cut out, it will continue rotting the very bowels of the nation.'

Then briefly he spoke of his own conversion and of his work in London during the plague. Dr. Sibbalds, the Protestant minister, interrupted: 'You ought not to glory in your good works.'

'I will glory in nothing', Morse replied, 'save in my infirmities. All glory I ascribe to God, who was pleased to make use of so weak an instrument, and this day is pleased to call me to seal my faith with my blood, a favour I have begged these thirty years.'

'You have now got your wish,' said the minister.

'Yes,' said Morse, perhaps for the last time fearful that he would show his vexation. 'And therefore I give the greatest praise I can to Almighty God. I pray that my death may be some kind of atonement for the sins of this kingdom; and if I had as many lives as there are sands on the sea-shore, I should willingly lay them all down for this end, and to testify to the truth of the Catholic faith. To this very day', he said once again, 'it is the only faith confirmed by miracles still continuing, by which the blind see, the dumb speak and the dead are raised to life.'

Then he addressed the sheriff.

'What say you, Mr. Sheriff? If you saw the dead return to life, would you not believe? Tell me,' he insisted, 'would you not say that it was the true Church where all these things are done? *For thy testimonies, O Lord, are made incredible exceedingly.*'

The sheriff ordered the priest to say his prayers in preparation for death.

He was silent for a few minutes. Then with his hands joined he prayed audibly.

'God eternal, Father, Son and Holy Ghost, most humbly I ask pardon for all my offences, for I confess myself a great sinner', and he mentioned especially his 'hastiness of temper', momentarily perhaps recollecting his exchanges with Fitton and Longeville. 'I repent from the bottom of my heart. As I pardon all those who have ever injured me, and especially those who now stain their hands with my blood, so I humbly ask pardon of all whom I have in any way offended.' Then he prayed 'somewhat more and interceded by name for Germany, Spain and France, and the other kingdoms of the Christian world, but especially for England, his dearly-beloved country.'

He then asked that his nightcap might be drawn over his eyes, for this was the custom, and he observed it in deference to his friends who were looking on. His own could not be found, but one of Egmont's suite came forward and offered his, giving two shillings to the hangman to ensure its return after the priest's death. Then he spoke those words uttered by many priests at Tyburn—*in manus tuas, Domine, commendo spiritum meum.* He struck his breast three times—the sign for a priest in the crowd to give him the last absolution. The cart was drawn away and Morse was left to hang.

Mercifully he was permitted to hang until he was dead. Seldom now was a traitor cut down alive as the sentence exacted. His clothes were stripped off, and for a few moments his body dangled naked from the noose. It was then laid on the block, and the sheriff, making a path through the crowd, invited the French Ambassador to approach to see the corpse quartered. Count Egmont also came forward.

'His bosom was then laid open,' wrote the Marquis de Sabran, 'his heart torn out, his entrails burnt and his body quartered.' When the butcher's work was done, footmen dipped their Ambassadors' handkerchiefs in Morse's blood. 'My Lords,' said Mr. Gibbs in shame, 'I regret that you should have witnessed such a spectacle, but such are our miseries that it must be done.'

That night the four quarters of the body were set on the city gates, the head on London Bridge. There are tears in the last page of Ambrose Corby's tribute.

'In the presence of an almost infinite multitude looking on in silence and in deep emotion, died Fr. Henry Morse, a saviour of life unto life . . . upright, sincere and constant. May my last end be like his.'

In Yorkshire Fr. Robinson received the news with similar emotion. Eight years later, after a further period of imprisonment in York Castle, he was arraigned and sentenced to death for his priesthood. With the other convicts, he was led to the gallows outside Micklegate Bar. But Parliament had hanged sufficient priests and sent a reprieve that reached York in time to save his life. 'I had hoped to be hanged, but in vain,' he wrote to the General of the Jesuits. 'What likelihood is there now that I shall follow Fr. Henry Morse, who was my fellow-prisoner twenty-six years ago when, as Zachary Vanderstyn, I received his vows? May he now be pleased to accept the prayers of his fellow-soldier.'

APPENDIX A

NOTE ON ILLUSTRATIONS

Facing pages 112 *and* 113

The first drawing shows a room in an infected house. On the left two persons are lying together in bed: one of them is vomiting. A figure (perhaps a doctor) is approaching. In a second bed, on the right, is another sick person; a woman, presumably a nurse, is carrying a dish towards her. Other persons, recovering but limping with their plague sores, are walking about the room with sticks. In the foreground is a body laid out for the bearers with a coffin close to it.

The second drawing shows a broader London street with a row of timbered houses, which are shut up, with a red cross marked on the locked doors and the bill 'Lord, have mercy on us!' below. In front watchmen stand on guard with halberds. In the foreground is a dog-killer: a raker is walking in front of him. He is pushing a barrow loaded with dead dogs. On the extreme left are two women searchers carrying large white wands in their hands; on the right two bearers are taking a sick person to the pest house in a covered sedan chair. Before every sixth house fires are burning.

The third drawing on this page and the first two drawings facing page 113 show bearers carrying bodies of plague victims (some coffined, others not) to a large graveyard outside the city walls and to plague pits in the fields. The uncoffined corpses are wrapped in shrouds and tied hand and foot. The bearers hold staves as a warning that all persons should avoid them. An open cart has just emptied its load of dead; the hooded cart behind is piled high with coffins. A procession of mourners, contravening the law, follows the corpse of a distinguished victim.

The last drawing shows the return to London after the plague.

APPENDIX B

SOURCES

Abbreviations: *C.R.S.*: Catholic Record Society; *S.P.D.*: State Papers Domestic; Foley: *Records of the English Province of the Society of Jesus.*

A. GENERAL

1. *Lives.* Two brief Latin lives of Henry Morse were written in the year of his death; *viz.*, *Certamen Triplex* (containing also the lives of Thomas Holland and Ralph Corby) by Fr. Ambrose Corby (Antwerp, 1645); and *Narratio Gloriosa Mortis quam pro Religione Catholica P. Henricus Mors . . . oppetiit*, by an anonymous author (Ghent, 1645). Both are concerned principally with the details of Morse's last imprisonment and death. Although the *Narratio* was translated into Flemish and French, the *Certamen* is more valuable. Alongside it must be placed two useful summaries of Morse's career in Fr. Matthias Tanner's *Vita et Mors Jesuitarum pro fide Interfectarum* (Prague, 1675) and Fr. Philippe Alegambe's *Mortes Illustres et Gesta* (Rome, 1657). Bishop Richard Challoner's short biography of Morse in his *Memoirs of Missionary Priests* (1742) is also valuable.

2. *Writings of Morse.* The English autograph of the extant section of Morse's diary covering his arrest and trial in 1637 has been lost. In the British Museum (Add. MSS., n. 21, 203) there is a Latin translation (eight pages) of this section, entitled *Acta Londini in causa P. Henrici Claxtoni a die Februarii a^i 1637 ad 24 Apr^{is} eiusdem anni ex eiusdem autographo fideliter desumpta ac latine versa.* This is the most important of Morse's writings. Another section of a journal, presumably translated into Latin, is in the Vatican Library (*Nunziatura d'Inghilterra*, t. 4, ff. 54–6). It covers his arrest on 17

June 1640, his appearance before the Court of High Commission and subsequent release. Two of Morse's letters are extant. The first, an autograph, undated and addressed to Fr. Fitzherbert from St. Omer in 1624, is in the Stonyhurst Archives (*Anglia*, iv, no. 67); the second, addressed to his Superior from Newgate in January 1645, exists only in a fragmentary translation into Latin printed in the *Narratio*. There are copies of the joint appeal of Morse and Southworth *To the Catholickes of England* in the Westminster Archives and in the Bodleian Library, Oxford.

3. *Secondary.* The only secondary source used throughout the book is Henry Foley, *Records of the English Province,* in eight volumes (1877–83).

B. Particular

Chapter 1. The background details of the execution are drawn from the news-sheets of the time, especially *A Perfect Diurnall*, no. 77, *The London Post*, no. 23 and *Mercurius Civicus*. For Morse's family the only source is the wills of Robert Morse and his children proved in the Consistory Court of Norwich. The MS. register of Corpus Christi gives the facts of his Cambridge career, the MS. Admonition Book of Emmanuel the details concerning Thomas Morse. *The Memorials of Father Augustine Baker* (*C.R.S.*, vol. 33) has been used for the pages on Morse's life at Barnard's Inn, together with his own verifiable statements under examination at Newcastle (cf. *inf.*). The *True and Wonderful. A Discourse relating a strange and monstrous serpent*, etc., is the pamphlet referred to on page 8.

Chapter 2. The *Douai Diaries* (*C.R.S.*, vol. 10) gives the dates of the arrival and departure of William and Henry Morse. The scene at Dover is taken from Foley, vol. 1, p. 217; the fact of his imprisonment from *S.P.D., James I*, vol. xcvii, no. 95. The extracts from Fr. Blount's letters are from a volume of Fr. Grene's *Collectanea* in Rome (Arch. S.J., Rome, *Ang.* 37). The date of Morse's release is taken from *Acts of the Privy Council* (1617–19), p. 197.

Chapter 3. The *Liber Ruber* of the English College (*C.R.S.*, vol. 37) notes Morse's arrival there and gives the names of his contemporaries. There are biographies of Fr. Fitzherbert in the *Dictionary of National Biography* and in Foley, vol. ii, p. 198 sq.; several articles in the *Venerabile*, the review of the English College, Rome, give descriptions of student life there; further details are found in Foley, vol. vi. A very large collection of papers deals with the troubles at the College: the most important are in the Westminster Archives (*Anglia*, viii, nos. 142, 148; ix, nos. 59, 64) and at the English College (*Scritt.* 29, v). The letter from Fr. Vitelleschi to Fr. Blount is in the Jesuit Archives in Rome, *Epp. Gen.* 1605–41, 1 (2).

Chapter 4. The sketch of Fr. Richard Blount is drawn from Fr. Henry More's *Historia Provinciae Anglicanae* (1660), Foley, vol. iii and John Morris, *Troubles*, series iii. The figures of the increase in numbers of the English Jesuits are based on MS. catalogues preserved at 31 Farm Street, W.1. For the organisation of the English Province, see Foley, vol. i, 98–141, and the papers assembled by J. G. Nicholls in the *Camden Miscellany*, vol. ii. Fr. Holtby's *Memoirs* are printed in *Troubles*, series iii. A full account of St. Anthony's can be read in *The Life of Mrs. Dorothy Lawson* (1851), written by her chaplain, Fr. Palmer. *Chorographia: or a Survey of Newcastle-upon-Tine* (1649), printed in the *Harleian Miscellany*, vol. iii, 267–84, has been used for local background. Lord Clifford's letter is in *S.P.D.*, *Charles I*, vol. iv, no. 46. Secondary sources are E. Mackenzie, *Newcastle-upon-Tyne* (1827) and R. Welford, *History of Newcastle and Gateshead in the 16th and 17th Centuries* (1887).

Chapter 5. The full classification of pursuivants in the north and the incident of the old woman robbed of her winding sheet are found in Foley, vol. i, p. 119 sq. The rest of the chapter is based exclusively on *S.P.D.*, *Charles I*: in vol. xxiv, no. 83, there is a sequence of eighteen papers concerning Anthony Vandenhaupt and Henry Morse; in vol. xxvi, no. 16, six papers concerning John Robinson. Bishop Neile's letter is in vol. xxx, no. 36.

Chapter 6. G. Minshull, *Essays and Characters of a Prison* (1618); T. P. Cooper, *History of York Castle*; J. Morris, *Troubles,* series iii (*A Yorkshire Recusant's Relation*); A. W. Twyford, *Records of York Castle* and *The Criminology of York Castle* have all been used. The incident of the conversion of the two criminals on the eve of their execution is taken from Fr. Grene's *Collectanea* (Stonyhurst MSS.) *N*.1. f. 77.

Chapter 7. The history of the Jesuit houses at Watten and Liège is drawn from Foley, especially the Annual Letters printed in vol. vii, pt. 2. P. A. Hamy, *Notes sur l'établissement et l'existence du Collège des Jésuites à Casel*, gives the few details about the house mentioned in the text. For Fr. Francis Line see Foley, vol. vi, p. 417, and his own notebooks preserved in the University Library at Liège.

Chapter 8. John Evelyn's *Fumifugium* (1661) has been used in the first pages, but the principal source for conditions in the London of Charles I is the *Middlesex County Records*, vol. iii; for the state of the streets, pp. 13–14, 226–8; night-walkers, p. 13; Peter Welsh, pp. 60–1; Henry Good, pp. 16–17; stocks in St. Giles, p. 12; Elizabeth Shipley, pp. 73–4; James Looker, pp. 11, 200. For the religious temper of the city, see, in addition, Père Cyprien de Gamaches's *Memoires*, translated under the title, *The Court and Times of Charles I;* for the scene outside the Queen's chapel, vol. 2, p. 243; see also W. Prynne's *Popish Royall Favourite* (1643). The incident of the Irish Dominican is taken from the *Historical MSS. Commission*, 4th Report, p. 355. Fr. Norton's letter to Fitton is at Stonyhurst (*Anglia*, viii, no. 199).

Chapter 9. See *S.P.D., Charles I*, vol. ccc, no. 31, for Sir Robert Parkhurst's letter; vol. ccci, no. 56, for the Earl of Arundel's Embassy; vol. ccciv, no. 46, for the Baron de la Ferté. Morse's retirement to Cheam is noted by Alegambe. The list of 'causes' of the plague is taken chiefly from *The Shutting-up of Infected Houses*, published in 1665 but drawn largely from observations made in

1636. The recommendations of the Royal College of Physicians were published in a pamphlet entitled *Certain Necessary Directions for the Cure of the Plague* (1636). The Plague Orders are contained in two other pamphlets: *Orders thought meet by His Majesty to be executed . . . in towns etc. inflicted with the Plague* (1636) and *Orders conceived and agreed to be published by the Lord Mayor and Aldermen of the City of London* (1636). The vagabondage in London brought about by the plague is described in a vivid and long letter of John Eliot to the Council, *S.P.D., Charles I*, vol. cccxxxiv, no. 28. Charles Creighton's *History of Epidemics in England* (1891) has also been used.

Chapter 10. Unless otherwise stated all the cases of individuals assisted by Morse are taken from *S.P.D., Charles I*, vol. cccliv, no. 31. The two quarrels between Southworth and Morse are narrated in Tanner and Alegambe. The names of Catholics who refused to contribute to parish funds are given in *S.P.D., Charles I*, vol. cccxx, no. 75. For the Protestant preachers, see Dr. Gouge's *Plaister for the Plague* (1636), *Royal Orders* (cf. chapter 9): for Mr. Sparrock, *S.P.D., Charles I*, vol. ccl, no. 54. Robert White's petition, containing information about Southworth's activities, is in *S.P.D., Charles I*, vol. cccxxxi, no. 93.

Chapter 11. For the condition of prisoners at this time, see *S.P.D., Charles I*, vol. cccxxii, *C.S.P.D.* (1636), p. 544. Dr. Gadbury's book is entitled *London's Deliverance Predicted* (1665). For Stephen Bradwell, see his *Physik for the Sickness* (1636): Samuel Speed advertised on the covers of a pirated re-issue of Kephale's *Medela Pestilentiae*. For restrictions on meetings and on the sale of 'stinking fish', see *S.P.D., Charles I*, vol. cccxxv, no. 26; cccxxvi, no. 9; cccxxxi, no. 43. The incident of the burial of Samuel Underhill is from *Middlesex County Records*, vol. 3, p. 62. For nurses, see Nathaniel Hodges' *Loimologia* (1672); for Dr. Turner and Dr. More, A. Wood, *Athenae Oxonienses* (1815), vol. 2, pp. 193, 326; also Gee's list of Popish Physicians printed in Foley, vol. i, p. 682.

cche story of Richard and Mary Seares is in *S.P.D.*, *Charles I*, vol.
Tcxlix, no. 116. For the rest, see Alegambe and Tanner.

Chapter 12. A few only of the very large number of State Papers
concerning Newton and his companions have been used: the most
thorough exposition of their practices are in *S.P.D.*, *Charles I*, vol.
cclxix, no. 55; cccxvii, no. 36; ccl, no. 75; and in Prynne, *A Popish
Royall Favourite*, p. 30 sq. The rest of the chapter is drawn from
Morse's journal.

Chapter 13. Morse's journal again is the principal source. There
is a record of the trial in *Middlesex County Records*, vol. iii, p. 112.
Newton's depositions and the petition of the officers of St. Giles are
printed in Foley, vol. i, from *S.P.D.; Charles I*, vol. ccxlix, no. 116.
The only description of Newgate at this time is in a letter of Edward
Rossingham to Sir Thomas Puckering (13 April 1636) quoted in de
Gamaches, vol. ii, p. 244. I have, therefore, made selective use of
later sources: James Whiston's *English Calamities Discovered*
(1696), in the *Harleian Miscellany*, vol. vi; *A Glimpse of Hell, or a
short description of the common side of Newgate* (1705); *A History of
the Press Yard* (1717). For Sir William Jones, see *Dictionary of
National Biography*. The letter of the General of the Jesuits at the
end of the chapter is from the Archives S.J. (Rome), *Epp. Gen.
(Anglia)*, i, (3), f. 455a.

Chapter 14. The incident of Con's intercession on behalf of
Morse is told in his despatch of 8 May 1637 (Vatican Archives,
Nunziatura d'Inghilterra, vi, 230). Foley (vol. i, pp. 587–9) prints
the report. of Fuller and Jenner from the Clarendon State Papers
(Bodleian Library) and (vol. i, pp. 606–7) the petition of Morse and
his two doctors from *S.P.D.*, *Charles I*, vol. cclxi, no. 20 and encl.
The description of Fr. Blount's funeral is from Greene's *Collectanea,
N.*, p. 16, at Stonyhurst. Fr. Morse himself describes his arrest and
appearance before the court of High Commission in a portion of
another journal preserved in the Vatican Library (cf. *sup.*). Incidents in London at this time are taken from R. R. Sharpe, *London*

and the Kingdom (1894), vol. ii. The letter quoted on the last page is in *C.S.P.D.* (1641) under 24 January.

Chapter 15. This chapter is based largely on *Alter Britanniae Heros, or the Life of the Most Hon. Knt. Sir Henry Gage* (Oxford, 1645). A manuscript concerning Peter Wright outside Salle is in the Academia de la Historia (Madrid), *Papeles de los Jesuitas,* vol. xxxii, no. 25. Wright's MS. sermons are at Stonyhurst. The *Annual Letters* of the Jesuit house at Ghent are in Foley, vol. vii, art. 2, p. 1197 sq. The funeral of Mrs. Lawson is described in her *Life* (cf. *sup.*).

Chapter 16. The first pages are drawn from *A True Relation of the Queenes Majesties Return out of Holland* (York, 1643); the Jesuit background from Foley, vol. iii. The story of Morse's arrest is based on the biographical sources. For Cumberland during the Civil War, see papers printed in the *Transactions of the Cumberland and Westmorland Antiquarian and Archaeological Society*, vol. xi (1891); for the war around Newcastle, *Archaeologia Aeliana*, vol. xxi. The prodigy in the sky on the King's birthday is reported in *The Scottish Dove* for Friday, 22 November 1644.

Chapter 17. For this and the following chapter all the biographical sources are very full. There are records of Morse's arraignment and sentence in the *Middlesex County Records*, vol. iii, pp. 94, 121; and of Susan Platt, *ib.* For Fr. Harvey, see Foley, vol. v, p. 556 sq. The escape from Newgate is described in a newssheet (1648) entitled *Strange and Terrible News from Newgate*; the death of Sir Henry Gage in *A Perfect Diurnall*, 13 to 20 January 1645.

Chapter 18. See general biographical sources. The details of the horse guards and the delay at Tyburn are taken from a letter of the Marquis de Sabran printed in E. Warburton's *Memoirs of Prince Rupert and the Cavaliers* (1849), vol. iii, p. 43n. Fr. Robinson's l etter is printed in Foley, vol. iii, pp. 57–8.

INDEX

Abbot, George, Bishop of London, 29

Abbot, Fr. John, 171

Alegambe, Fr. Philippe, biographer of H.M., quoted, 17, 21, 22, 55, 57, 58, 60, 61, 80, 81, 87

Allen, William, Cardinal, 7, 10

Allen, Margaret, plague-victim, visited by H.M., 86

Almond, Fr. John, 6, 174

Angel tavern, Long Acre, reputed headquarters of the Jesuits, 74

Anne of Denmark (wife of James I), 30

Anne of the Ascension, Mother, 177

Appeal, made jointly by H.M. and Fr. Southworth, 89–90

Ark, takes Fr. White to Maryland, 67

Arundel, Countess of, 74

Arundel, Earl of, 77–8

Arundell, Lady Blanche, 13

Bailey (witness at H.M.'s trial), 129

Baisty, Thomas, 2

Baker, Augustine, O.S.B., 5–6

Baldwin, William, visited by Fr. Southworth, 96

Ballard, Mr., 92

Bambrigg, Edward, 48

Barnard's Inn, 5, 47

Bartendale, John, 59

Beazly (a porter), 2

Bedingfeld, Fr. Henry, 63

Bedingfeld, Henry, 8

Bedingfeld, Margaret, 8

Bellarmine, Robert, Cardinal, 19

Bemean, Richard, 173

Brereton, Sir William, 162

Berry, John, 45, 51

Berry, Thomas, 49

Biggs, John, 127

Bills of Mortality, 107

Bishop, William, Bishop of Chalcedon, 31

Blackstone, Sir Thomas, 39

Blount, Fr. Richard, 13, 28 ff., receives Earl of Dorset into Church, 30; secretly visits the Queen (Anne of Denmark), 30; 44, 45, 67, 72, 75, death, 141

Bonfires, a remedy for the plague, 82

Borwick, William, 56–7

Bradwell, Stephen, 102–3

Bridlington, 158

Broome, Suffolk, 3, 4, 47

Browne, Fr. James, 171

Bucher, Alexander, 14

Bunney, Edmund, 55

Calendar, Earl of, 164

Campion, Fr. Edmund, referred to, 17, 34, 94

Canam, Fr. Edmund, 171

Capcot, Dr. John, 5

Carew, William, 45, 46

Carlton, Sir Dudley, 98

Cassel, 61

Catholic doctors in the plague, 101–2

Catholic funeral service, in secret, 106

Cawan, William, 56

Charity Mistaken, by Fr. Matthew Wilson, 73

Charles I, 2, at Hampton Court, 85; petitioned by debtors in Fleet prison, 99; orders sentence on H.M. to be deferred, 136; receives report of George Con, 137; gives orders to Windebank to suspend sentence on H.M., 138; H.M.'s letter to, 139–40; orders H.M. to be released, 140; promises proclamation against Jesuits, 147; raises standard at Nottingham, 153. *See also* Charles, Prince

Charles II, visits English College at Liège, 66; praises Fr. Lusher, 135

Charles, Prince, proposed marriage to Spanish Infanta, 14, 31; negotiations break down, 39; marriage to Henrietta Maria by proxy, 40. *See also* Charles I

Cheam, Jesuit house at, 80; watched by Thomas Mayo, 117

Chichester, John, 142

Chillingworth, William, 72

Christ Church, Oxford, 2

Christopher Ultan, Fr., Irish Franciscan in Newgate, 180

Christ's Hospital, 142

Claxton, Henry, *see* Morse, Henry

Claxton, Sir John, 39

Clifford, Lord, letter to Council, 35, 141

Clink (prison), plague deaths in, 99

Coke, Sir Edward, 6

Coke, Sir John, 116, 123, 124, 136

Cole, Ralph, 44

Coleman, Fr. Walter, 171

Collinson, William, *see* Morse, William

Collinson, Margaret, mother of H.M., 3

Con, George, 137–8

Constable, Sir Henry, father of Mrs. Dorothy Lawson, 32

Conway, Lord, Secretary, 51

Conyers, Mr., 45

Cook, John (pursuivant), 113, 116, 118 ff., 126, 138–9

Corby, Fr. Ambrose, first biographer of H.M., 21; quoted, 58, 62, 174, 176, 185

Corby, Catherine, 62

Corby, Brother Gerard, 62

Corby, Mary, 62

Corby, Fr. Ralph, 62, 159

Corby, Fr. Robert, 62

Cornwallis, Lady, 144, 146

Corpus Christi College, Cambridge, 4–5

Council, complaint to Archbishop Laud, 85; petition to, by parishioners of St. Giles-in-the-Fields, 112; orders inquiry into conduct of pursuivants, 138

Courtenay, Mr., 142

Courtney, Fr. Edward, 26, 65–6

Coventry, Thomas, 6

Crowe, Cecily, assisted by H.M., 96–97; testifies at H.M.'s trial, 134

Dann, John, 43, 45, 50, 51, 52

Darell, John, 32

de la Ferté, Baron, 77

de Melo, Don Francisco, 151

de Sabran, Marquis, 177, 181

de Santa Cruz, Marquess, 149

de Sousa, Don Antonio, 182

Dodd, Charles (historian), quoted, 18

Donne, John, 84

Douai, 8, 9, 10, 11, 14, 16

Dover, bitterness of religious feeling in, 12

Downes, Fr. Edmund, 20–1, 63

Dunkerque, 9; plague at, 77

Edmonton, Jesuit novitiate at, 32, 45

Egmont, Count, Duke of Guelders, 169, 182, 185

Ellesmere, Lord, 6

Emmanuel College, Cambridge, 3

English College, Rome, 5, 18–19; strife at, 22 ff.

English Regiment in Flanders, 153

Erasmus' *Dialogues*, 6

Evelyn, John, quoted, 68

Eye, Norfolk, 4

Fairfax, Sir Thomas, 2

Fairfax, Thomas, 43, 44, 48

Falkland, Lord, 72

Falkner, Fr. John, 13
Fawether, Sir James, 3
Fenner, Sir Gregory, 144
Fisher, Fr. Philip, 73
Fitton, Fr. Peter, 22–3; expelled from English College, Rome, 24; intrigues in Rome, 25; clergy agent in Rome, 75; instigates dispute between H.M. and Fr. Southworth, 94
Fitzherbert, Fr. Thomas, 17–18, 22–3, 142; letter from H.M. to, 25–7
Flanders, 3; war in, 61 ff., 148 ff.
Fleet prison, debtors given liberty, 99
Flying Hart, 42, 43
Fortune, 49
Frederick Henry, Prince of Orange, 61, 148, 152
Freeman, Bartholomew, 117
Freshwater, Edward, assisted by H.M., 92
Freshwater, Mrs., 110
Fryer, Fr. Andrew, 171
Fuller, Henry, 138
Fuller, Thomas, quoted, 39–40

Gadbury, Dr., quoted, 100
Gage, Henry, 148 ff.; death, 172
Gage, Lady, 92
Gage, Thomas, 150
Garnet, Fr. Henry, venerated at English College, Rome, 24; referred to, 31
Gascoigne, Fr. Thomas, 159, 161
Gatehouse prison, Westminster, 98; plague deaths in, 99
Gee (spy), quoted, 29
Gerard, Fr. John, referred to, 63, 64, 75, 135; quoted, 34, 35
Ghent, Jesuit house at, 150–51; English Convent at, 154
Godwin, Elizabeth, assisted by H.M., 92
Gondomar, Count, 16
Good, Henry, 71

Goodman, Godfrey, Bishop of Gloucester, 143
Goodman, Fr. John, 143, 145, 146–7, 171
Gouge, Dr., quoted, 93
Gray (pursuivant), 117, 129, 131, 143, 171
Gregory XV, statements to, from factions at English College, 22–3; death, 24
Greyhound (Parliamentary ship), 158
Guelder, siege of, 151

Hales, Samuel, keeper of York Castle, 54
Hall, Bill, 56
Hall, Mrs. Frances, 110, 129, 131
Hambley, Fr. John, 7
Hammond, Fr. John, 171
Hart, John Johnson, 42, 43, 44
Harvey, Fr. Thomas, 175–6, 179, 180
Hastings, Walter, leaves Rome with H.M., 25; lent money by H.M., 26
Haywood, William, Rector of St. Giles-in-the-Fields, 110, 124
Hebburn, 32, 47
Henderson, Fr. William, 171
Henrietta Maria, wife of Charles I, arrives in England, 40; contributes to relief of plague victims, 92; buys back seized vestments, 116; hears George Con's report of H.M.'s trial, 138; obtains H.M.'s release, 140; returns to England from Holland, 157; shelters from bombardment, 158
Heywood, Fr. Jasper, 34
Hodges, Dr. Nathaniel, quoted, 109–110
Hodgson, Sir Robert, 32, 43, 44, 48, 51
Holland, Cuthbert, 109
Holtby, Fr. Richard, joined by H.M., 32; work in the north-east, 34–5, referred to, 45, 57, 159

Holywell, 31

Hugget, Mary (prisoner in Newgate), 172

Inns of Court, 3, 6, 7, 8

James I, 14

Jarrow, 32

Jenner, Edward, 138

Jesuits in England, their numbers in the time of Fr. Blount, 30; their disposition, 31; number in London, 72, 73; reputed organization, 73–4; numbers in north of England, 159

Johnson, William (apostate priest), 42

Johnson, Yorkin, 49

Jones, Sir William, 132, 133

Kellison, Dr. Matthew, 10, 16, 17; referred to, 45

Kephale, Richard, pamphlet by, 97

Knott, Edward, see Wilson, Fr. Matthew

Lambe, Sir John, 142

Lanherne Carmel, 177, 181

Latham, Fr. Edward, 150

Laud, Archbishop, receives complaint from Council, 85; signs warrant for H.M.'s removal to Newgate, 125; questions H.M., 143; flees to Whitehall, 144, 169; sentenced and executed, 171

Lawson, Mrs. Dorothy, 32 ff., 52; visits H.M. in prison, 53; daughters in convent at Ghent, 154; her funeral, 154

Lawson, Henry, 48

Lawson, Sir Wilfrid, 162

Leedes, Fr. Edward, see Courtney, Fr.

Liddel, Thomas, mayor of Newcastle, 47

Liège, 23, 26, 60, 63, 64, 65, 66, 73, 141

Line, Fr. Francis, 66

Lloyd (pursuivant), 117

Lobb, Fr. Emanuel, 20

Longeville, Fr. Thomas, 22–3; penance imposed on, 24; helps to arrest H.M., 142

Lowe, George, quoted, 113

Lusher, Fr. Edward, 73, 122, 134, 135

Maastricht, siege of, 149

Maidenhead, 84

Marston Moor, 164

Maryland, 67

Mass, celebrated in shrines, houses and prisons, 7, 8, 31, 38–9, 55, 96, 169, 179

May, Lady, 92

Mayo, Thomas (renegade priest), 117, 150, 171, 173

Medela Pestilentiae, by Richard Kephale, 97

Mercurius Britannicus (newspaper), quoted, 171

More, Fr. Henry, 139

More, Dr. John, 101, 140

Morse, Anne, eldest sister of H.M., 4

Morse, Edward, brother of H.M., 4

Morse, Geoffrey, brother of H.M., 4, 11

Morse, George, brother of H.M., 168

Morse, Henry, S.J., birth and parentage, 3; early education, 4; bequest under will of his brother Lionell, 4; at Corpus Christi College, Cambridge, 4–5; his hot temper, 5; at Barnard's Inn, 5–7; first religious scruples, 7–8; at Gray's Inn, 7; leaves for Continent, 8; at Douai, 9–10; received into Church, 9; confirmed, 11, 30; returns to England, 11; bequest under will of his father, 11; arrested and imprisoned at Southwark, 12–14; banished to France, 14–15; at Douai, 16; at Rome, 17 ff.; friendship with Fr. Fitzherbert, 18;

strife at English College, 22; leaves Rome for England, 25; letter to Fr. Fitzherbert, 25–7; in Switzerland and Germany, 26; at Watten, 27; received by Fr. Blount in London, 29; at Newcastle, 32 ff.; boards *Sea Horse*, 45; ordered ashore and held prisoner, 46; examined, 47–48; taken to prison, 48; joined by Fr. Robinson, 51; visited by Mrs. Lawson, 53; transferred to York Castle, 53; absolves condemned criminals, 56; makes *Spiritual Exercises*, 57; released, 58; arrives at Watten, 60; ministers to troops, 61; falls ill at Cassel, 61; appointed Minister at Watten, 62; supervises Passion Play, 64; transferred to Liège, 64 ff.; returns to England, 67; works in St. Giles-in-the-Fields, 69 ff.; appointed to administer relief funds during plague, 79; retreat at Cheam, 80; visits plague victims, 86–7, 108; censured by Fr. Southworth, 88; joint appeal with Fr. Southworth, 89–90; praises Protestants, 90–1; his 'faculties' questioned, 94; falls sick, 95; ordered to rest, but recovers, 101; arrested, 110; questioned and released, 111; visits pest-house, 113; arrested by John Cook and purchases release, 114; visits retired pirate captain, 117; arrested by Newton and Cook and taken to Westminster, 118; instructs servant to inform the Queen, 119; bargains for release, 120; surrenders to Newton, 122; brought before Privy Council, 124; removed to Newgate, 125; ministers to prisoners, 127; trial, 129 ff.; found guilty, 134; makes solemn profession in prison, 134; sentence deferred, 136; letter to the King, 139–40; medical report, 140; released, 140; works in south-west of England, 141; returns to London and re-arrested, 142; appears before Archbishop of Canterbury, 143; ordered back to Newgate, 143; released, 145; goes to Continent, 146; chaplain in Flanders, 148; returns to England, 157; works in the north, 159; captured, 162; escapes, 163; recaptured, 166; sent to London by sea, 3, 167; in Newgate, 169; writes to Provincial, 170; sentenced to death, 174; visited by Ambassadors, 177; celebrates Mass, 179–80; journey to Tyburn, 181; dying speech, 182–184; execution, 1–2, 184

Morse, John, brother of H.M., 4, 11

Morse, Lionell, second brother of H.M., 4

Morse, Margaret, sister of H.M., 4

Morse, Martha, sister of H.M., 4

Morse, Mary, sister of H.M., 4

Morse, Philip, brother of H.M., 11

Morse, Robert, father of H.M., 3; his will, 3, 11; death, 8; delated as a recusant, 8

Morse, Robert, 4, 8, 11, 168, 169–70

Morse, Thomas, 3, 5, 11

Morse, Fr. William, 8, 10–11, 12, 16, 17, 141, 175

Morse, William, Master of Trinity Hall, Cambridge, 3

Moryson, Fynes, 9

Neile, Richard, Bishop of Durham, organizes search, 51

New Prison, 12

Newcastle, 1, 3; increase of Catholics in, 35; plague in, 36, 161; description of city, 36–7; coal trade, 37; glass manufacture, 38; salt, 38; grindstones, 38; fear of assault by Catholics, 39; re-enforces fines on recusants, 39; collapse of coal trade 160; siege of, 161; surrenders, 165

Newcastle, Marquess of, 158
Newcastle-under-Lyme, 14
Newgate, 2, 125 ff.; prisoners escape from, 174; visitors to, 174–5
Newgate prison, Newcastle, 53
Newport, Fr. Richard, 6
Newton, Francis, 116 ff., 126, 129, 131, 137, 138–9, 142, 145, 150, 170, 171, 173
Newton, Isaac, 66
North, Mr. (alias of Fr. Holtby), 43, 44
Norton, Fr. Benedict, 75
Norwich Grammar School, 4

Oldcastle, Sir John, 71
'Orthodox Sam' (chaplain at Newgate), 128
Osborne, Dr., of Corpus Christi, Cambridge, 5

Parham, Sir Edward, 149
Parker, Matthew, Archbishop, 4
Parkhurst, Sir Robert, Lord Mayor of London, 77
Parsons, Hugh, sentenced to *peine forte et dure*, 172
Pennington, Sir Isaac, 146
Persons, Fr. Robert, 17, 24
Pirate captain, 117
Plague, in Newcastle, 36; in Pont-à-Mousson, 36; in London, 40, 78, 106; in Dunkerque, 77; in Flanders and Germany, 77; infected houses shut up and watched, 79; relief measures organized by Catholics, 79, 89, 92; alleged causes of, 81; remedies for, 82, 88, 102–3; rats, 82–3; symptoms of, 88–9; reaches peak, 100; burials, 106–7; number of deaths, 107; sick-nurses in, 107 ff.
Platt, Susan, 173, 174
Pope (watchman), 129
Potter, Christopher, 73
Providence (Parliamentary ship), 158

Prynne, William, 116
Pulford (pursuivant), 145
Pursuivants, 14, 35, 41–2, 115 ff., 137

Resby, Lady, 92
Robinson, Fr. John, at Rome with H.M., 20, 45; arrested under name of Zachary Vanderstyn, 49 ff.; transferred to York Castle, 53, 56; appointed H.M.'s novice-master, 57; sentenced to death, 58; receives news of H.M.'s death, 185
Rochester, Fr. Thomas, 159
Rocroi, battle of, 151
Roger, Fr. Thomas, 20
Roper, Philip, 139
Ross, Richard, 7, 11

Sackville, Thomas, Earl of Dorset, 30
Scott, Fr. Montfort, 8
Scott, Fr. William, 6
Scottish Dove (newspaper), quoted, 166
Sea Horse, 44 ff., 50
Seares, Richard and Mary, 110
Sheppard, Thomas, *see* Morse, Henry
Sherwood, John, 4
Shipley, Elizabeth, 71
Sick-nurses in plague, 107 ff.
Simpson, Fr. Christopher, 159, 161
Smith, Fr. Ralph, 24–5
Smith, Richard, Bishop of Chalcedon, 94
Somerset House, Queen's chapel at, 72
Southampton, Earl of, 69, 70
Southern, Fr. William, 14
Southworth, Fr. John, 76, 79; censures H.M., 88; makes appeal with H.M., 89–90; watched by Robert White, 95; arrested, 98; continues work in prison, 99; referred to, 105, 108, 112
Sparrock, Mr., quoted, 93
Speed, Samuel, 104
Spencer, John, 118, 120

Spiritual Exercises, 45, 57, 64, 80, 150

St. Anthony's, Northumberland, 32, 38–9, 43

Steward, William, 49

St. Giles-in-the-Fields, description of, 69 ff., 78; plague in, 78; lawlessness in, 83; sealing-up of infected houses, 86; pest-house in, 87, 113

St. Leonard's Forest, 8–9

St. Omer, 20, 26, 28

Storie, Robert, 56

Strafford, Earl of, 147

Stuston parsonage, 8

Styles, William, visited by Fr. Southworth, 96

Swan, Dudley, 46, 47

Swan, William, 43, 46, 49, 51

Syer, Edith, 11

Symonds, Sir John, 92

Tanfield, Sir Lawrence, 6

Taylor, John, quoted, 84, 104

Taylor, John, *see* Robinson, Fr. John

Thresher, John (pursuivant), 142–3, 145

Tivetshall, Norfolk, 3, 11

Treatise on the Barometer, by Fr. Francis Line, 66

Tresham, Fr. Edward, 171

Tresham, Thomas, 149

Tromp, Admiral Martin, 157

Tuelmont, sack of, 152

Turner, Thomas, Catholic doctor, 95, 101–2, 104, 140, 169

Tyburn, 1, 14; Irish Dominican executed at, 73; John Biggs hanged at, 127; H.M. at, 181

Urban VIII, 24

Vandenhaupt, Anthony, 42 ff.

Vandersteggin, Francis, 50

Vanderstyn, Zachary (alias of Fr. John Robinson), 49 ff.

Vanderswain, 50

van Middelen, Fr., 62

Vaux, Lord, of Harrowden, 10

Vavasour, Sir Thomas, 59

Vitelleschi, Fr. Mutius, General of the Society of Jesus, 25, 134

Wadsworth, James (pursuivant), 117, 173

Wallis, Fr. Francis, 65, 141

Want of Charity, by Christopher Potter, 73

Ward, Mr., leaves Rome with H.M., 25; lent money by H.M., 26

Wardour Castle, 13

Warner, Fr. Christopher, 25

Warner, John, plies barges during plague, 85

Watten, 20, 27, 28, 45, 60–1, 63, 65

Webb, Robert (constable), 124

Westminster, pest-house in, 87; plague mortality in, 95

White, Fr. Andrew, goes to Maryland, 67; quoted, 68

White, Robert, watches Fr. Southworth, 95; secures his arrest, 98; referred to, 112

Widdrington, Roger, 159

Wilford, Fr. Peter, 171

Williamson, John, 56

Wilson, Fr. Matthew, 72–3, 79, 134, 135, 169, 170

Winchester House, 2

Windebank, Sir Francis, 66, 140, 145

Wright, Fr. Peter, 150, 152, 154, 172, 179

Yarmouth, H.M. visited by brothers at, 168

York Castle, 53 ff.

Young, Robert, 44